I've travelled the world twice over,
Met the famous: saints and sinners,
Poets and artists, kings and queens,
Old stars and hopeful beginners,
I've been where no-one's been before,
Learned secrets from writers and cooks
All with one library ticket
To the wonderful world of books.

© JANICE JAMES.

TIME REMEMBERED

Born just before the First World War, Ralph Finn grew up in London's vanished East End Jewish community. His mother had been a schoolteacher in Russia, his father a scholar in Poland, but in the new country she ran a stall and he pressed clothes for twelve hours a day. Life in Broughton Buildings was hard — rats and bugs, dirt, crowding — but rich in character and experience. There were the Choots and the Polaks: the anglicized Jews and the recent immigrants from Eastern Europe, the Chocolate King in the street market, and Cockneys calling their wares in Yiddish. This autobiography conveys the spirit of this unique world.

RALPH L. FINN

TIME
REMEMBERED

Complete and Unabridged

ULVERSCROFT
Leicester

First published in Great Britain in 1963
under the title
'No Tears in Aldgate'

First Large Print Edition
published 1996

British Library CIP Data

Finn, Ralph L. (Ralph Leslie), *1912* –
Time remembered.—Large print ed.—
Ulverscroft large print series: non-fiction
1. Finn, Ralph L. (Ralph Leslie), *1912* –
2. Jews—England—London—Social life and
customs 3. East End (London, England)
—Social life and customs
I. Title
942.1'5'004924

ISBN 0–7089–3515–X

Published by
F. A. Thorpe (Publishing) Ltd.
Anstey, Leicestershire
Set by Words & Graphics Ltd.
Anstey, Leicestershire
Printed and bound in Great Britain by
T. J. Press (Padstow) Ltd., Padstow, Cornwall

This book is printed on acid-free paper

The imagination of a boy is healthy, and the mature imagination of a man is healthy; but there is a space between, in which the soul is in a ferment, the character undecided, the way of life uncertain . . .
John Keats (Preface to *Endymion*)

Foreword

A few months ago I received a rather bulky letter. The writing on the envelope was only vaguely familiar. When I opened the envelope out dropped a worn and sad-looking autograph album. And my heart missed a beat. I knew that little blue book. Many, many years ago it had been part of me.

The letter was from an old schoolboy chum who, in this book, I call Harry. I had not seen Harry in years . . . long, crowded years that had rushed by and swallowed up our youth, our early manhood and our maturity. Now, suddenly, the years were wiped out and we were back again, boys together.

My fingers faltered as I held the letter. It read: *My dear old friend,*

A voice from the past — almost the dead past. You may have heard that I was gravely ill. As a result I had to tidy up things and on going through mountains of debris found two things, one a surprise, which gave me great pleasure.

The first thing was a charming letter you sent me after my mother died ten years ago. The other I enclose. God knows how it has survived thirty years!

I read it with blurred vision, I must confess. And I am sure it will give you nostalgic pleasure to have the commonplace book back again after virtually a lifetime.

It is unlikely that we shall meet again, so I now wish you goodbye and a long and pleasant journey in the happy uplands.

Sincerely,
Harry

I cried. And the sight of the autograph album with its snatches of quotations from the poets side by side with bits of doggerel and childish whimsy did not help me to control my tears. Why was I crying? For Harry . . . for the lost years . . . for the wonderful colourful exciting struggling sad mad and glad past. For days that were gone that would never be again. For those like Harry and all the inhabitants of Broughton Buildings who were once alive and strong and exultant.

And I thought: I am still a comparatively young man, unold anyway. Yet so many of those I knew are dead or dying. Time took its toll of some. The war of most. And they have no memorial, except in my thoughts and in the remembrance of others. Who knows where Broughton Buildings stood? Who wants to know? Who cares? Does anybody care as I care?

And I thought: but people will care. This is a part of the living past that, with the inspiration of men like Harry at my elbow, I can bring back to living reality.

And so this book was born as an idea. Thinking in the clear uncluttered thought of those days, I have used the phraseology and the expressions then current. I have not set out deliberately to be indecent or sensational, but I have refused to alter the words that we then spoke — to have done so would have been distortion and deceit.

If some of my tales are a little outspoken, a little too close to the gutter, I can only say that that is where we lived. Yet out of this garbage came great men — politicians, architects, musicians, painters, writers, teachers, scientists, research-workers, fighters, doctors, lawyers — men like Harry whose contribution to journalism helped towards building the world's largest-selling newspaper, and others who have made their mark in the world of art and science.

To have altered the words we used or the thoughts we thought or the sights we saw, to have varnished sex and gilded behaviour, would have been cheating: a betrayal of the men who were boys when I was a boy.

Of those now dead I have altered only the perhaps still recognizable name. Of those still alive I have written with care and discretion, hiding their lights under bushels that will prevent their being discovered by all but me who planted them.

Everyone in this book existed. No, exists. For me they can never die.

RALPH L. FINN
London 1962

For Freda, who knew the East End well; Alan, who has begun to know it too late; and Andrea, who will never know it as it was.

For winter's rains and ruins are over,
And all the season of snows and
  sins;
The days dividing lover and lover,
The light that loses, the night that
  wins;
And time remembered is grief forgotten,
And frosts are slain and flowers
  begotten,
And in green underwood and cover
Blossom by blossom the spring begins.
Swinburne: *Atalanta in Calydon*,
Chorus

1

In the Beginning

I REMEMBER very little before Broughton Buildings.

I remember my father sitting wrong way round on a chair and leaning against it and sending me to buy him a penn'orth of acid tablets.

I remember him carrying me over his shoulder out of a Fever Hospital and home. There I was put on a sofa and everyone came in to look at me. I had forgotten how to talk.

I remember washing my hands at the sink one day when there was a heavy rumbling in the street. And I rushed out crying "Daddy's coming . . . daddy's coming", knowing he had been long in hospital and that he was due home. And I saw the long line of black cars and the black box and my mother following after the cars and screaming and tearing her long fair hair. I was three years old.

I remember coming down one morning soon afterwards to play with my baby brother, Louis, asleep in his cot. And being pushed gently aside by my mother. And again the long line of black cars, the crying and the sobbing and my mother tearing her hair.

No angry young man, I. Death I knew well. It came early into my life.

Then I remember our moving to Broughton Buildings. We had taken two flats, each of two rooms. One flat rose out of the basement where all the dirt and dust and refuse of fifty flats lay after it had been shoved down slots on each of six landings of the tenement. Our other flat was just above, just above floor height, atop the one below.

I remember the crowds of children and adults watching as the men tried to get our big old-fashioned piano up the stairs to that first-floor flat. And how a leg broke and the crowd roared its glee. Forever after the piano stood on one unchanging carved leg. The pile of books that held the balance changed frequently.

Then we were in. The upstairs show

flat. The downstairs warehouse.

For my mother had a barrow — a stall as it was known — in Goolden Street, the street which housed Broughton Buildings. And the things on the stall were each night carried into the downstairs back room, the room which looked out on Goolden Street, and each morning carried out again.

My Zaida — grandfather — slept in that back downstairs dark room with all the bits of glass and china in crates, the beads and baubles in trays, souvenirs of the Coronation of George V — gilt bits of cardboard and flags — and the poles around which were wrapped the tarpaulins that covered the stall.

There was never any light in this room. Never any air. The windows always remained tightly shut and curtained, first by fabric then by grime. It was cluttered with the junk of the stall, all the bits and pieces a family acquires in its years of living, spare bedding, broken furniture and my Zaida's bed.

The front room housed my Booba — grandmother — and the kitchen stove, a dresser, a table and some chairs.

The Broughton Buildings flats were made up of two rooms and a narrow scullery running off them that contained the gas cooker half-way along, with a sink at the far end. Next door to the sink was the W.C.

Because we had two flats — in the eyes of Broughton Buildingites we were therefore very rich — we turned the downstairs front room into a kitchen. There Booba held sway, cooking and preparing for all of us.

Upstairs in the back room immediately above the room in which Zaida slept, my mother, and sisters Polly, Betty and Lily slept. In the front room, immediately above the kitchen, my brothers Edward, Mark, Ben and I slept.

Both flats were distinct. You left one and went out on to the general stairway and down or up eight stairs again till you reached the second home. You were under cover all the way, but only just.

The green exterior doors opened straight into the front rooms. People therefore slept in the back rooms that overlooked Goolden Street. There were too many of us to follow suit. So the upstairs front

4

room was a parlour by day, with cleverly hidden sofas, ottomans and put-u-ups that converted at night into beds for the male brood. And in the morning we all set to to turn the beds back again into couches.

Downstairs, in the basement, there were rats. Not just mice, but rats. And bugs. Upstairs in the show rooms there were just bugs. Legions of them.

Now and again a denizen of one of the upper flats would heave a dirty old mattress out over the landing and into the yard below. And the bugs would start running out in wide red streams like blood from the flanks of a pic-ed bull.

But the bugs never really worried us though they bothered us. I used to wonder as a child how many bugs there were in Buckingham Palace. I could not conceive of any place in the world being bug-free.

Thus, you can see that I never really suffered the agonies of poverty and hunger because I did not know I ought to have been suffering.

Of course we were poor. Sometimes hungry. Sometimes with big holes in our boots and socks, and feet that were wet and black because we had no baths — once a week we used the public baths across the street. But I thought this sort of poverty was a natural hazard of being alive. Common to all, I supposed.

And when the angry young men came on the scene and were angry about all that they had *not* suffered, I could only feel angry with *them*. For if they had known one war, we knew two. If they had known hard times, they could not have known the devastating poverty of the thirties, the unemployment and the real hunger. If they were complaining about bad living accommodation, how many of them took bugs for granted or had known the horror of rats scampering across their bed at dead of night?

I am getting angry now and demonstrating a reversed inferiority complex. They have names for everything today. You can't fart without being analysed and particularized and shoved into a pigeon hole.

But angry with the conditions of my childhood? That I was not — as a child. In fact, I often went with

6

friends to the neighbouring districts of Shoreditch, Hoxton, Bermondsey, Canning Town; up the Commercial Road to Custom House and Plaistow; to Millwall, Rotherhithe, Limehouse, Wapping, Shadwell and Bethnel Green to see *the slums.*

We called those places slums. We had no idea at all that we also lived in one. Not for years did I realize that I too had been born and had lived till the age of seventeen or eighteen in a slum.

Maybe the fact that most of Broughton Buildings was Jewish territory had something to do with it. With Jews, children come before beer. And kids tended to be better dressed and better fed than their kind in equally unsalubrious areas.

Come Passover, for instance, and every kid in the place would have a new suit or dress. The Passover Parade could be observed as one kid after another self-consciously came down to take his or her place in the posturing groups standing around.

Come the normal Friday evening and we cleaned up for Sabbath. And though our families were poor there was always a bottle of wine on the table. How did we do it? We didn't spend our money in the pubs. Fathers who worked sacrificed everything for their wives and kids. Mothers slaved, went short themselves, but the kids ate.

For many years I thought the pubs were a deliberate invention of the upper classes to keep the lower British classes poor. And happy in their poverty. It's not such a bad thesis when you consider it, is it? Certainly the pubs caused more misery in my young days than any other wickedness or depravity I can think of. Wages were squandered there before they were earned. Men went home drunk to terrify their families. Prostitution flourished in them. Gambling was rife. It was masculine territory in those days and no decent women went near them. And they were the breeding grounds for more unhappiness than the poverty which made them popular or the ignorance which kept them in business.

Let's face it. Intelligent people in those days did not frequent pubs.

Nice people didn't. They were the home from home of the loutish, the stupid, the ignorant, the intolerant — the salt of British democracy! Long live the working-class sots!

2

Paved with Gold

BROUGHTON BUILDINGS was to be my home for some fifteen years and I suppose it was this environmental factor that, combined with my hereditary one, helped to mould me into the soured, embittered introvert this writing shows me to be, much to my own conscious astonishment.

From the breeding point of view I had much to be thankful for. Father had been a scholar in Poland. Mother a school-teacher in Russia. Their villages were not more than half a mile apart and frequently they did not know, as sovereignty switched, whether they were Russian or Polish. Perhaps they preferred being Poles because they couldn't stand those Russian winters.

Going back, they could both trace their lines through a long line of scholars. Zaida, my grandfather, was a Levite;

a member of the tribe of priests. His family name was Lev. He and Booba, my grandmother, were my mother's parents. Mother brought them with her when she came to London in 1900. At that time only my eldest brother Edward existed. He was Russian born. The rest of us were born in the East End of London. True if not true-blue British.

The unbroken line of scholarship on both my parents' sides differentiated us almost immediately from most other immigrants who had known years of oppressive uneducation. These people were not ignorant. Some of the wisest men I have met were ancient Jews who could not read or write. They fathered world-famous musicians, writers, thinkers. The intelligence was there. It was not their fault that education had not been given them.

My family had been lucky. In the villages of Russia and Poland in those days the scholar was the responsibility of the community. He did not work. He sat in the synagogue and studied and read and taught. And people came to him for advice and instruction. Sons followed fathers in this calling. The villagers brought food and clothes. Wisdom and learning were so highly respected that it was considered a *mitzvah* (a good deed) to reward it by keeping it alive. I believe the Buddhist priests live much the same way.

Father had shown signs of being an architect. He was drawing flat-roofed sun-trap houses years before anyone in Britain had even thought of houses built this way. "Go to England, Alec," they told him. "The streets are paved with gold."

He went alone sending for mother and Edward and mother's parents a year later. When they found him he was living in poverty near the London Docks. No one would look at his work. He had been laughed at. To keep body and soul together he had taken up clothes pressing. He, the man who had never wielded anything heavier than a pen all his life, stood by a heavy iron and pressed and breathed damp hot steam and sweated twelve hours a day. Have you ever seen a Jew with a spade in his hand? O my poor father! And O you sons of Israel who make the desert blossom! How do you do it if not with spades and heavy press irons and the heart beating fast?

He was already sick when mother was reunited with him. His heart had begun to fail. He lived on for nine years. Fathered six more children. Died. My mother was heart-broken. He was thirty-eight when he died. She, thirty-five, blonde, tall, well-made, attractive. But she never married again. She devoted the remainder of her life to looking after her parents and caring for her brood. She, the educated genteel young schoolmistress, unable to find work in an alien land, took to a barrow and eked a living from the sale of junk. And somehow she gloried in her debasement and managed to extract from it the last ounce of kudos. Everyone knew her story — how much she had sacrificed, suffered, endured. And that she had been made for better things. She told them, glorying (it seems to me now) in her suffering and emoting over her devotion. In fact she enjoyed being a triton among minnows. She loved the worship and adoration of the less intelligent and, though she was kind to them, I'm convinced that part of her despised them for their ignorance. In her own world, among her equals, mother would never have been the power she was: the power she loved to be. And without that she could never have been the woman she was. So her misfortunes were not entirely unfortunate.

By birth, then, we had much in our favour. Our environment made us tough. Tough, not in body, but in mind. Aware of evil, depravity, wickedness, hunger, sorrow, misery; aware too of the innate goodness of most of the people around us, even the worst types. We knew the risks that had to be run in the process of living. And ran them gleefully.

Goolden Street, which ran parallel with Petticoat Lane and was an extension of the market, was on one side a street of tenements: Broughton Buildings. The length of the street was trisected by three blocks, in each of which there was an arched entrance. Through this arch you came to an open playground bounded by area railings. The tenements went right down into the areas and rose up sheer

14

into the sunless sky.

The middle archway, where we lived, was the most exclusive because it gave access to only one tenement whereas the top and bottom of the street archways led into huge playgrounds that housed ten and more perpendicular masses of grey stone, hundreds of poky flats, thousands of people.

Your little world was your own arch with its own yard and buildings. The archways were connected at the far end by narrow alleyways yet, for all the going and coming between them, they might have been separated by a range of mountains. Each separate archway with its enfenced playground was alien territory.

Above and beyond these localized divisions there were other vast cleavages of race, religion, colour and profession.

The greatest difference lay between Jew and Jew. The foreign Jews, the more orthodox of the community, were called *Polaks*. Whether you hailed from Rumania, Hungary, Austria, Belgium, Russia, Bessarabia, Lithuania or Latvia you were a *Polak*. And if you were the offspring of immigrants you were a *Polak* too.

Those born in England and their children, second generation English were known as *Choots* (the "ch" rolled as in "loch"). *Choot* was a generic term for Dutchmen. Practically all Jews who were not immigrants had settled in England some fifty years before and had originated mainly from Holland, some from Spain and Portugal.

The *Choots*, being more anglicized than the *Polaks*, were less orthodox. They ate *traife*, forbidden food. They loved their jellied eels. They drank beer. They lived by gambling. Most of them were either bookmakers or employed by bookmakers. And they struggled along till greyhound racing came to Britain. Then they went to the dogs and grew rich.

The *Choots* children did not go to *Cheder*, Hebrew classes, in the evening, and very few went to the Jews' Free School. The segregation, you see, extended even to education. *Choot* children went to the local city schools like Gravel Lane.

Prostitution, always rare among Jews,

was — where it existed — confined entirely to *Choot* women and girls. "Foreign" females never went bad. Family ties, much stronger than in the anglicized *Choot* households, kept the *Polak* females in check.

All the *Choots* seemed related. If you fell foul of one of the *Choot* boys he would stand in the centre of the playground and yell: "Aunt Marfy! Aunt Marfy!" and there would descend a horde of slovenly unkempt women led by the shrewish witch of a woman they called "Aunt Marfy". Spoiling for a fight, swearing like troopers, these women, often as many as twenty of them, would take up their charge's quarrel. God help you if you stayed to argue. These harridans would have your hair out by its roots and tear your clothes from your back.

The *Polaks* never stayed to argue. They ran and shut themselves within their houses and stayed quiet till the row had simmered down. Not until the Warsaw Ghetto battle did *Polaks* stand and fight. And then they showed the world they could fight and die. It was better that way than the torture rooms and the gas chambers.

Among forty or fifty families in our centre archway tenement there were only two *Polak* families. We learned early on to avoid trouble. And there were less scenes in the centre archway than in the other larger more mixed communities.

Because I was naturally good at games I made friends quickly with the *Choot* lads. Once on terms petty differences were soon forgotten. A ball was a great keeper of the peace. Moreover, the Choot women soon learned to love my mother and respect Booba and Zaida. "Mrs. Alec" as they called mother — it was the custom to call married women by their husband's Christian name — was different. They instinctively knew she was different and somehow better than they; and all Mrs. Alec's brood were therefore entitled to consideration.

My mother became known as "The Philosopher of Petticoat Lane". One national newspaper called her that and ran a story about her. She not only wrote letters in six different languages for all those immigrants with families still abroad, and translated the replies when they came, but gave advice freely, settled disputes, adjusted differences, brought quarrelling husbands and wives together, and was the peacemaker, correspondent and mother confessor all at the same time. And never charged a farthing for her troubles. But she got more than money from all this — she practically bought the indebtedness of people and almost paid for adoration. And how she loved to be worshipped.

People in the Buildings called her *Die Schreiberkie* — the Writer — and as her fame spread so did the crowds around her barrow increase until it was a wonder she ever sold anything at any time.

Then the leftovers from the groups around the barrow would follow her into our upstairs parlour and there they stayed, talking, arguing, listening to mother, and eating our grub.

Mother, who had been brought up in a scholarly Jewish house, knew the Bible almost by heart and the talmudic and rabbinical books too. She could quote at will. And words of learned length and thundering sound amazed the rustics ranged around, especially as mother could quote in the original Hebrew. And usually did.

By the time I was seven I had a fund of Biblical quotations picked up at mother's knee. Jews like to talk. They love a good talker. My mother was queen-empress of all she surveyed. And how she revelled in the role!

3

First War

I WAS but two years old when the First World War began.

I remember little of its early days. But I do recall running into the yard reading a newspaper and shouting aloud the bold headline: *Russia Surrenders.*

"Rushuh suhrrenduhs . . . Rushuh suhrrenduhs!" I yelled aloud and brought crowds running.

I remember the air raids too. Every inhabitant of every flat would crowd into our first-floor front room. The basement was considered unsafe. "Torpedoes" the wise ones whispered. The top flats were obviously perilous. And when everyone was scared out of his or her wits there was Mrs. Alec, calm and dignified, ready to tell a joke or a story, or even to start a sing-song, to soothe and comfort frayed nerves.

Zaida could not bear crowds. He used

21

to take me by the arm and lead me out into the playground to watch the fireworks in the sky. When we heard a bomb falling we would throw ourselves flat on the stone floor, I ever ready to follow my leader and do as Zaida did. He could do no wrong in my childlike eyes.

We saw the first big zeppelin shot down in flames and watched it fall across London. We listened to the anti-aircraft fire and the bombs and though I was scared I was also thrilled and excited and knew that while Zaida was with me we could come to no harm.

But one night he shouted at me in Yiddish to get down quickly and, as I threw myself on the floor, a bomb burst not very far away, and a lump of shrapnel whistled by our heads, struck the area railings with a resounding clang and ricochetted back to crash against the far factory wall.

Zaida and I went to look for it. Zaida found it. It was a shining piece of metal about as large as a hammer top, and about as big and heavy. Zaida picked it up gingerly with his red handkerchief. It was still hot.

The area railing where it had first found a mark was bent out of true and a huge chip had been carved in its painted shininess; and out of the playground wall it had also chipped a sizeable lump before coming to rest.

This was the last time we went out at night. Mother forbade further excursions.

I remember Armistice Day vaguely but knew that mother did the best day's trading she had ever done in all her life. She sold the stall clear of all it possessed and all the flags and gewgaws she had left over from the Coronation of George V, all the golden paper scrolls and cardboard crowns and coats of arms, went like wildfire.

Zaida complained bitterly that we would have nothing left to sell any more. When I think of that I think with a smile of the story of the two Jewish dealers who, over the years, bought and sold the same clock to one another, always the same clock. Until one day one confessed sadly that he had had a good bid for it and had actually sold it. To which the other replied, tearfully: "And how shall we live now you've taken our

23

bread and butter away?"

I remember the hot summer of 1921, when I was nine, and the never-ending days that, even then, seemed to drag on. And the General Strike when our teachers came to school in an array of patched-up old cars and decrepit bikes. And the afternoon we were sent home because a thick fog shadowed all and the lights were not working.

But most of all I remember my Meccano box in which I kept wheels, pinions, gear wheels, sprockets, chains, clips, screws and all the more vital and more expensive parts of the set I had been given and to which, over the years, I had added part after part till it had become quite some set.

I used to save my halfpennies and pennies until I could afford one wheel, or just one bright part and then, on Sunday mornings, would be off to Wolfs, the toy shop at the top end of Middlesex Street, to make my purchase.

All my spare money went on buying extravagant and rare parts. And I kept them all in a carved grey box, a jewel box it must have been once, for it was dark blue silk lined and looked exactly like a miniature pirate's chest. Mother gave it to me off the stall. I treasured it. I adored its contents *en masse* and worshipped them each separately.

In Zaida's dark room, the back room down in the basement, the one that fronted Goolden Street and was separated only by the height and depth of the area and its railings from mother's stall, there amid the junk that overflowed from the stall, for which barrow-space could not be found or for stuff that could not be sold, there in a shelf against the wall I used to hide my precious box.

One afternoon I came to play with it and it was not there. I turned the room inside out. I had Booba and Zaida sharing my search. Everyone helped. The box was not to be found. I cried as I had never cried before. I was nearly eleven, I suppose.

For weeks after that I resumed the search each evening, and at weekends. The loss was an emptiness in my heart. Something irreplaceable had gone. I hadn't the money and if I had, I would not have had the same feeling for replacing my gems. All the joys and patience and agonies of hope and anticipation and yearning were in that box. All a collector's pride in his rare specimens.

The weeks passed into months and I slowly gave up the search. I never played with my Meccano set again. I couldn't.

So I grew out of childish toys and was getting on for manhood when the day of our leaving Broughton Buildings arrived.

And there, as the junk went out and the shelves came down, wedged between far shelf and wall was the precious box.

I opened it with fingers that trembled with the memory of the way I used to open it so many years before. There they were, all my pieces, lying snugly in the blue silken covering. Every wheel, every pinion as I remembered it.

Years, years too late. Years of growing from boyhood to early manhood. Long years of stage by stage development out of imagination into reality. Years of remembrance and death. Loved ones, dear ones gone, while that box remained safe in its obscurity.

As I held that box in my hands again after such a long lapse of time I began to cry. I, who had grown ashamed to weep, cried softly, nostalgically, for all the days that had been, for my lost toys and my lost youth and all the long, lost, lost, lostnesses of those days.

I shut the box tight, went out into the street, and put the little treasure chest into the hands of the first urchin I saw. He looked at me with eyes that were wonder lit and opened the box and gaped and said incredulously: "For *me*, mister?" It was the "me" that did it. My eyes brimmed with tears again and he turned and ran away clutching the box to his little chest.

And to this day I don't know which of us was the more delighted, he thrilled by his unexpected gift or I, light heartened into joyous weeping by his radiant face and ecstatic happiness.

I saw Broughton Buildings again once or twice during the Second World War. The kids were still there in the playgrounds singing, but not "One, two, three O'Leary" any more.

Now they sang, to a popular catchy tune of Disney's:

> *Whistle while you work,*
> *Hitler is a twerp,*
> *Mussolini's*
> *Got no penis —*
> *Whistle while you work.*

The balls still went down the area and intrepid youngsters who should have been evacuated, had been, probably, and had drifted back, clambered after them or up the concrete factory walls to retrieve them.

Some of the people we knew were still there. The call of "Aunt Marfy!" still brought a horde of rather more ancient-looking women down to the playground to protect their brood.

My mother's stall wasn't there, of course. But there was a fruit barrow of the man who was to be able to boast, soon, that his grandson, Alfred Marks, was one of Britain's best comics.

And there were one or two of the prozzies, now definitely whores and no mistake about it, either.

And then, a few weeks later, I heard about the bomb and I hastened down to see Broughton Buildings.

It was no more. The bomb had done its work well. A heap of stone and rubble contained what was left of Broughton Buildings. Many of the people in this tale and many more I have not even mentioned died with it.

For me that was the end. The end of my first period of living.

Leaving Broughton Buildings had not entirely cut all ties. But this had. This was the finish. The old world was dead. Bury the dead past. When I am dead, my darling, sing no sad songs for me.

Again, O yes again, and how often, so often in these years since, the past came back to possess me. Broughton Buildings where I had lived for more than fifteen years of my life was gone.

Gone, and by the bombs of heaven destroyed, home of my early days, stay bodiless as you are, better lost and forgotten, better thus, remembered only as a child remembers, than alive, sinfully, excitedly, exultantly, wickedly, thrillingly, ecstatically, alive.

Gone, and by bits of earth symbolized, precious years of early living. Gone and your pulse stilled and your heart uprooted and your sinews torn to shreds and all the wheels of being scattered. Dust to dust. Rubbish to rubbish. Dirt to dirt. Bugs to blood. Garbage to ashes.

Weep not for the days that have gone, nor for the long nights under rooms crammed with the living bearing down upon your head; weep not for lost days, nor for the people, living, breathing, loving, nor for the people. Weep not for them, but remember them a little, with kindness if you can, with mercy if you dare. Weep not for the people, but think of them now and again. Only in your thoughts have they a memorial, in your dreams their glory of immortality.

Only in your thoughts. Only in you. Who else remembers? Who else cares?

4

First School

JEWS' FREE SCHOOL was my first primary school.

It was then the largest school in the country. It had six floors, each with its own hall, miles of corridors, a roof playground, three lower open playgrounds and three more under cover, the largest ground grand main hall I have seen then or since, and at least a thousand boys.

Next door, the girls' school was almost as large. The staff of both departments was unusually competent, qualified and kindly.

It had produced great scholars. Lord Reading, Rufus Isaacs, Viceroy of India, had, I believe, been a pupil there. Israel Zangwill was also one among a distinguished group of surgeons, professors, lawyers and rabbis who had graduated from the school.

The staff, brilliantly qualified but

academically thwarted because of the large numbers of stupid scholars that were to be found in a school of this size, greeted the bright boys with open arms and showed them all sorts of favours. In the A classes life was sweet.

I entered the school with some trepidation but need not have worried. My ability could not be disputed. And as I moved from class to class I knew that the teachers had passed on the good news of my coming. This encouraged the growth of the ego within me and much of my overweening conceit can be traced to the fact that I was an infant prodigy — and everyone let me know it.

Maybe I therefore thought I could get away with more than most. I don't remember ever thinking so, but I can't otherwise find a rational or satisfactory explanation for what occurred.

I was in the Scholarship class. There we were favoured with a different master for each subject — the only class in the school thus rewarded by specialized tuition.

My form master — sorry, class teacher — who took us for English had said he would eat his hat if I didn't get through. In those days the winning of a Junior County Scholarship was a tremendous achievement. Schools took a half holiday to celebrate when a pupil gained such an award. I like to think of this tall grizzled man eating his hat.

I did not get the Junior County. But, a year later, when I was in the Central School, an upper department of the so-called Graded School, I won an Exhibition Scholarship and on going to the Grammar School found that the Junior County winners were all bottom of the class. So much for examination ability.

But to get back. For Maths, a white-haired little man, a brilliant teacher, took over. He didn't invent crosswords but he devised them from the outset for the London "Star" and went on compiling them, daily, for many years. He had that sort of clear, logical, mathematical mind.

I thought he liked me. I was not a badly behaved lad. I worked well. I made few mistakes. And I was top of this class in Maths as in English.

Mr. Star (I shall call him) gave us a test one day. I finished early and sat back twiddling my thumbs. The boy sitting below me — the classrooms were staired in broad lanes of ascending steepness — asked me the answer to a sum. I wrote it on a piece of blotting paper and passed it down.

Star looked up and caught me.

"Come out!" he said.

I expected a tirade, a scolding. I expected to be accused of cheating and to have an opportunity of denying it. I didn't think I was cheating then and I don't think so now.

But he didn't say a word.

He motioned me, by putting the cane under my wrist and jerking it upwards to raise my hand.

One.

I felt awful. I had never been caned before. It wasn't the hurt; it was the indignity.

Two.

Both hands felt hot and stinging.

But Star was coldly, diabolically merciless.

Three.

Four.
Five.
Six.

He put his stick down. The class was silent, awed, horrified. As for me I wanted desperately to cry. But I never made a sound. I went back to my desk and clasped my sore, throbbing palms round the cold iron stanchions of the desk. The pain was awful. I thought it would never go away.

When I could bear to look at my hands the palms were all puffed and angrily swollen and it was torture to touch the tight, tender skin.

Six. For what? Why?

Six. Six, six, six, six, six, six.

Each stroke cut deep into the heart and brain and deeper still into the unconscious processes of growth and development of a young boy.

I was eleven. I had never really been hit as hard as that in all my short term of living. My mother did not hit me at all. Zaida and Booba certainly didn't. Occasionally one of my brothers or sisters would cuff me. At *Cheder* I had been boxed on the ears.

But the cane? Never. Even the news of one stroke would have horrified my mother. Six would have sent her round to the school demanding to know what had happened.

I never said a word to anyone. The boys in the class did not talk to me about it. No one called after me in the street. Somehow everyone seemed to know an injustice had been done.

Alone, I nursed the grievance. Six was a terrible punishment. Had a boy had the temerity to cheek Mr. Star or even hit him, I could not imagine his getting six. Truants did not get more than a couple. A boy who had stolen the class library funds had only had two. I had never even seen six given. Now I'd got them.

Six of the best. I couldn't understand it. Had I really been cheating I reckoned that *one* was the most other teachers would have considered fit punishment. Cheating was an everyday affair in this school as in others. It was natural to cheat. I had seen cheats punished. Never very heavily. Teachers did not take cheating seriously. Often the culprit got away with a scolding.

What had got into Star? Why had he shown his personal hatred of me by giving me six? What had I done to annoy him?

This is how I reasoned then. Today, as I look back, I think he must have been ill or worried or angry. And he took it out on me. I was his catharsis for some terrible wrong.

For next day he went on treating me as he always had done. He stood over me when marking my work and overtly acknowledged his pleasure at the correctness of it. And neither by word nor gesture did he hint that I prompted any hatred or vexed him in any way. But my hatred was a wound to my pride and the scar would always throb. The punishment left a trauma that was to fester and suppurate all the days of my life.

What should I do? I had to get even. I thought of nothing else for days. Then I decided to show him up. To make him look foolish. To prove I did not have to cheat. And the way to do it was to be so bright, so clever, so outstandingly intelligent that he would have to admit, to himself if not to me, that a boy of such ability had no need to cheat.

So I worked harder than ever in that year. I listened to every word of every lesson; and when I caught myself day-dreaming, the scribbled '6' all over my blotter would soon pull me out of day-dreams and back to the classroom.

Painstakingly I did my homework. If he asked for the first twelve sums, I gave him twenty. If he went on, in class, to work we had not done before, I knew all the answers, having (with my brothers' assistance) worked ahead of the class by many chapters.

At the end of the year I took every single prize in the class — for Maths, English, Geography (which Star also taught), History, Science, Scripture, Hebrew — the lot. Even for Art.

The Jews' Free School was well endowed. In addition to book prizes for each subject and a couple of books each for the first three top boys, there were bigger and better awards donated by the Montagues, Montefiores, Franklins, Sassoons, Rothschilds and the old, aristocratic and famous well-breeched Jewish families of the days before Bernhard Baron, Woolfson and Clore.

In my own year there was a prize for the best of the eleven-year-olds. There was also a special prize for the Junior School. I took them both. I set up a record which stood (till the school was bought by the Houndsditch Warehouse Company) of being the boy who had taken most prizes in any one year.

The big hall. Crowded with people. A host of distinguished men and women on the platform. And the prize-giving. And my name being called fifteen times. Up and down I went till I was laden with books, till three volunteers from the audience were summoned to help me and the hall rang and rang to the most phenomenal prize gathering ever seen.

When I finally came down from the hall with the clapping still about me. I had to pass the front line of seats on which sat the staff in all its glory. And Mr. Star came forward to pat my head and say something encouraging.

I sensed in a moment, with that

awareness that the young often have, that he was wanting to show me off to his less fortunate colleagues on the front bench who had not had the delight of teaching me. He was getting kudos out of my feats. He was playing into my hands. I had waited a whole year for this moment.

I turned to him, looked into his periwinkle blue eyes, and said loudly: "Six of the best!"

Then I knew he remembered. Now I realize that he had a conscience about it, too. He had not forgotten, although at the time I was so sure he had.

For he took a step back, his face blanched, he dropped the books he was holding and suddenly he sat down heavily on the chair while masters and boys rushed to pick up my books and the noise interrupted the proceedings on the platform.

And then I found those lost tears. They fell from my eyes like long pent up rain, heavy and fast. And he, crouched up in his seat and bent, was crying too. Now was the time for the grande gesture. Now he should have jumped up and put an arm about me and told me he was sorry. Or I should have commiserated with him.

I looked at him and he looked at me and both our eyes were red rimmed and neither of us said anything more.

When I wandered back to my family they thought I was crying for joy. My mother was crying. My sisters were crying. Everybody was happy. When Jews are happy they always cry.

But the wound of Star's six of the best could never be healed by tears. I had been misjudged. The world was far more evil than I thought. Things were not just plain black or white. One had to be cautious or one was trapped, suffered punishment one had never deserved.

The wound was slow in healing. I doubt if it has ever truly healed.

5

Lonely Joy

I ENJOYED solitude.

I loved the rain falling, the deserted streets, the reflections of shop windows shining through rain-polished pavements. I was near to tears when petals fell. I comforted myself with pathetic fallacies of my own tortured making. Best of all I loved sitting on top of a 'bus at twilight watching the summer rain just beginning to fall. It made me so sweetly melancholy, so forlornly satisfied.

Even today I love the rain falling in quiet streets as day changes to dusk and the world wraps itself in tears and sadness. There is in me that feeling for wistfulness that the deep notes of the violin seem best able to call forth and the slow sombre slanting of rain best able to accompany.

When I was five and six and seven I

wandered through the East End streets singing sad songs to myself — *sat sonks*, as the Russian impresario of that wonderful entourage that used to come here in the late 1930s was wont to say.

I remember I would sing to myself:

*I get so blue through and through
When the leaves come tumbling
Down from the trees . . .*

because its plaintive melody touched some inner cord of anguish within me.

So, just because they made me feel sad, and for no other recognizable reason, I wallowed in sentimental ditties.

Sweet Sue was another one of my favourites.

*Every star above
Knows the one I love —
Sweet Sue,
Just you . . .*

Singing this, I could imagine myself suffering the pangs of a fierce and tremendous love. *We climbed the lane*

43

together, Laughed at the rain together
had me all moist-eyed and tremulous
with suppressed emotion.

Even the mawkish affected me. I could
ring tears at such banality as:

Sometimes, oh how I long for you,
I'm so terribly strong for you,
That's why I've written this song for
  you —
Nobody's fault but your own.

Even today I can recall every word
of every song and every poem I ever
learned. To me was given the great gift of
finding music in words and, once found,
of never forgetting. It was a gift which
was to stand me in wonderful stead all
the days of my life.

At school it put me way in front of
everyone. I could remember when others
forgot. There was nothing clever in my
remembering. But just as most people
can remember the subject that most
profoundly takes their fancy — some
go for football players' names, others
for racehorses and still others for public
houses — I went for word music. Given,

at eighteen, Tennyson's 'In Memoriam' to study, I could recite the long poem that made a small volume right through from beginning to end. Every chunk of Shakespeare I ever had to study remains in the memory still, every out-of-the-way poem and song. The good and the bad alike. The great gift was not selective. It just remembered.

Today, when so many old songs are being revived, I can always surprise those around me by recalling every word of every line. My memory is a storehouse of quotations and snatches of song and it needs only a nudge for them to come spilling forth in remembered delight.

Had the gift run to History, Geography, Science and Mathematics, to equations and formulae, I might have been brilliant. But I had only this small gift. And for this I have been ever grateful.

My brother Mark had an equal facility for going to a show or musical comedy and emerging with every quip remembered, every song perfectly recalled. He became a Marx Brothers fanatic — he can make himself look like Groucho, his favourite — and would return from a Marx

Brothers film romp with every crack trembling on his lips.

My sister Betty who was, when young, a pretty good dramatic actress (so much so that Moscowitch, the great actor of the 1920 – 30 period, when he heard her, prophesied a brilliant stage career for her), could also learn verse quickly. She was particularly good at Shakespeare and could recite almost entire plays. When she was cast in a school play she not only learned her own part but everyone's, not because she tried to but because, by oft repetition, the words stuck in her as they would do in me.

Theda Bara we used to call her at home. Theda Bara was then the great Hollywood star. And Betty's acting ability did not forsake her in the home.

Betty never became an actress. In those days the stage was still not an honourable profession. It was a far far better thing to work as a secretary in some dignified office.

Mother was a great story teller. She had a remarkable memory for old folk tales and obscure rabbinical tales. And she could sing songs as old in story as the Jewish tradition itself.

I was being continually surprised in later years as I found writer after writer rising to fame on the telling of stories I had heard at my mother's knee. Even Somerset Maugham's famous story of the verger who couldn't sign his name and grew rich and when asked what he would have been if only he had learned to write replied, 'A verger' . . . even that tale was told to me years before Maugham rewrote it.

Popular songs by the score came drifting over the air to me as the years went by — songs I had hummed as a babe, echoing the tunes heard from mother, Booba and Zaida's lips.

Somewhere along the line I, had I had the supposedly Jewish eye and ear for business, could have made a couple of fortunes putting words to tunes I knew. Since I had in the course of time put words to what seemed to me far more important things and since I had a fair acquaintance with music, the task should have been comparatively simple. And I did think of it once or twice, especially when a song I had been singing for years suddenly flared into popularity with ridiculous words, or a story I had heard told better by mother suddenly hit the headlines as a brilliant original gem of storytelling.

But I never did make any profit out of a richly storied childhood. Not that I had any scruples. Believe it or not, with all my inheritance I just lack the business instinct.

So, whenever I was by myself, I was happy in my solitude. I sang to myself the songs of the day or repeated aloud the more poignant pieces of poetry that lingered in my ear. O aching time! O moments big as years!

And then, one day, someone gave my brother Ben and me jointly a little brown mongrel pup, and the days of my solitude were over.

The pup had large liquid brown eyes, a plump little brown body and the most appealing ways in the world.

We doted on it. We fed it. We bathed it. We patted it off to sleep in the downstairs back room where Zaida slept.

Brownie, we called it.

For weeks it filled our young lives with

all the unforgettable excitement of its being there to greet us as we came home from school, *Cheder*, or boys' club . . . of its just being there to welcome us.

We were a little bit starved of love, I think. Mother had the stall. Zaida his synagogue. Booba her chores. Our brothers and sisters their friends and jobs. We were rarely fondled. I often earned praise but I rarely won an embrace. And the same, I think, went for Ben.

We were an affectionate family, but we were not demonstrative. We seldom made a fuss of one another. Mingled with our Jewish emotions was a sort of northern reserve that was peculiarly foreign to our kind of Jew. Even our Russian ancestral streaks did not give us free rein to express our emotions. We all seemed to feel deeply and clamp those feelings tight. Mother emoted a lot. She went into hysterical outbursts. My sisters could lose their tempers and rant. But when it came to showing affection we were singularly shy.

But Brownie was a safety valve for Ben and me. We cuddled him, embraced him, fondled him, fussed him.

Saving our ha'pence, we bought him a lead and collar. It was funny to see the brown little bundle of fur being hauled whither be wot not and wanted not by one or the other of us. Sometimes by both.

Then one day we found him moping. He wouldn't eat. He lay in his box and looked at us out of his big brown eyes. His nose was dry and hot.

We wrapped him in a blanket and took him to the People's Dispensary for Sick Animals.

Distemper, they said. They offered to destroy him.

Horrified, Ben and I refused to think of such a thing. We would make him better. Our Brownie should live. Would live.

We went home, put him to bed. Gave him hot water bottles, spoon-fed him forcibly, thrust pills and medicines down him at the prescribed times.

But he grew no better.

And one long night we sat with him, refusing to go to bed, and watched him die.

At the last he lifted his liquid brown eyes, those soulfully liquid eyes, at us

50

and sighed deep and was dead.

Brownie had gone. How we cried.

We wrapped him in the blanket and stole out in the early morning mist that lay over the East End like a shroud and went down to the river and there alone and silent in the vastness of a sleeping city we threw his lifeless body into the water and turned away and cried our sad way home.

I never kept another pet.

In the growing up, in the loin-stirring stretches of puberty, in nights of fevered tempestuous passion-paining dreaming and days of frustrated inhibited agonizing imaginings, manhood came.

In the days of adolescence life suddenly lost its savour; yet, with it all, there was a greater awareness of little things, a sadness that left the door open for poetry, a sorrow that music could accompany.

In the teens, he then thirteen, fifteen, a youth verging towards manhood, it was nostalgia and the haunting dreaminess of sentimental melodies, and knights on shining steeds chasing the Holy Grail of pure love and bandits on wild horses capturing the ecstasies of impure love.

In the growing up it was all mixed up.
In the youthful years it was purgatory.

6

Petticoat Lane

ON Sundays Goolden Street became an overshoot, an offshoot, a branch of Petticoat Lane. It ran parallel to Middlesex Street (which is Petticoat Lane, in case you didn't know, and is called Middlesex Street because it marks the boundaries of the City of London in Middlesex with the East End which is Essex. Policemen on one side of Middlesex Street wore the City police uniform, spiked hats and slightly different tunics; on the other, the usual London police uniform was worn. And a man could get drunk or involved in a brawl on the Essex side of The Lane in full view of the Middlesex policemen on the other side, and they did nothing about it. And vice versa. I have seen prozzies thumbing their noses and making all sorts of rude gestures at police on the wrong side of the road).

On Sundays Goolden Street became alive. It was crowded from stem to stern with stalls and barrows, elbow to elbow with people. And O, the cries and the colour and the excitement. This was the golden road to Samarkand, second on the left as you pass Aldgate Pump.

Every Sunday without fail, from the time I was five till the time I was sixteen and more, I made my tour of The Lane, beginning in Goolden Street, working through the side turning that connected it with Middlesex Street, up Middlesex Street and back through Goolden Street. A studied tour, incorporating as it did a stop at most of my favourite stalls, took the best part of the afternoon. Progress was slow. And the attraction of some stalls had a never-ending fascination for me.

I soon got wise to the chocolate kings, but continued to watch their slick operation.

Having drawn the crowd, thrown out a few jokes, a few just as mouldy sweets, they went into their big spiel.

They piled boxes of chocolates on boxes of chocolates, sweets on sweets, nougat on nougat (*nugget*, as we used to call it then).

And they cried: "Here's a box of Oberon, making number one: a box of famous Cornish creams making number two; this — making number three; that — making number four." They held in their hands a mountain of eye-watering confectionery, about ten or twelve gaily coloured boxes of near-famous assortments. Near-famous, because the names on the boxes were cunningly reminiscent of well-known brands, popular makes. Perhaps only a letter was changed. "Codbury" for instance, instead of "Cadbury", "Fray" for "Fry". Even more cleverly done, in fact, for the change was not obvious, the market men kept to the well-known pronunciation, and the lettering and colouring had been printed to resemble the original packets.

From a distance it seemed that the crowd was being offered a range of the best confectionery of the day. Come, taste of the fruit of the Tree of Knowledge. Taste before you buy.

Then came the real moment.

"I want ten sportsmen to come forward.

Come on now, ladies and gentlemen. Ten sportsmen. I promise you it won't cost you a penny. In fact, you're all in for a wonderful surprise. Come on now . . . you sir — what about you, sir? It won't cost you a penny. Come on now . . . !"

And led by the market man's stooges a few people would step forward and the market man would go on shouting the odds until he had as many as the crowd would yield, a dozen, twenty, thirty mugs. His first cry for only ten was by now forgotten. Besides, who bothered to count?

"Now," he would say, surveying his victims, "will you put a ten-shilling note on top of one of those piles? I promise you it will come back to you. I don't want your money. I'm not selling this stuff, I'm giving it away!"

Not selling this stuff — giving it away. It was the slogan of the market. Run when you hear it. Back to your houses. Pray to the gods to intermit the plague that needs must fall on such stupidity.

Gullible as the public were and are and always will be, they hesitated before committing themselves to ten bob. It was a lot of money in those days when a weekly wage of thirty shillings was as much as most men saw for a fifty-hour week.

But the stooges, cleverly planted, always solved this difficulty. First one, who had not been among those stepping forward, would politely tender his ten-shilling note and would be just as politely told: "Sorry, sir . . . not you, sir . . . only these sportsmen here before me. Too late, sir. You know what happens when you're too late? You shit the bed!"

Raucous laughter. Then the second stooge out in front with the rest of the mugs would gingerly place his ten-shilling note on top of the heaped piles of mock confectionery.

"That's the way, sir. You're a real sport, I can see that. Come on, I'm not taking your money. You'll get it back. I'm not selling anything. I'm giving it away. What about you, sir . . . and you . . . and you?"

Soon there are ten-shilling notes on top of every pile. Twenty or thirty piles with twenty or thirty separate ten-shilling notes placed above them.

"Now . . . " — the great moment, the climax to the build-up, the moment of sale — "who will give me ten shillings for the boxes of one and two and three and four and so on, and, *and*, AND the ten-shilling note with them? Eh . . . ? Wait a moment! Don't all rush! I know I'm giving it away. I told you I was, didn't I? But you didn't believe me. Thought I was one of those slick market thieves you read about (nice touch this). Now you all want to grab. Sorry. I'm sorry, gentlemen. Your turn will come. It's first come, first served here. And these ladies and gentlemen in front of me have first claim. If they'd like to give me ten shillings for one of these magnificent piles each containing twelve boxes of the finest assortment in the land *and* a ten-bob note for free . . . they've got first option. I told you I was giving it away . . . ten shillings, that's all I ask for these wonderful boxes AND the ten shillings on top that I give you, free, gratis and for nothing . . . "

On he went, keeping the mugs dangling with a psychology born of long experience in the market and then, at the crucial moment, he clapped his hands.

"Right . . . who's first?"

The stooge was always first. But the mugs were not far behind, each tendering his ten-shilling note for about a dozen boxes of confectionery and a ten-shilling note.

But in all probability it wasn't till they got back to their little houses and found themselves ten shillings short that they worried as to what really went on at the Chocolate King's stall.

And I doubt if any of them ever realized that they had bought their own ten bobs back and had, in fact, given ten shillings for what, when they opened it the following Christmas, turned out to be mouldy, soapy chocolates, the cheapest of boiled sweets, toffee that took the teeth right out of your gums and marzipans made of boiled elastic. The contents of the boxes were worth less than the boxes themselves. The lot was bought by market men for a couple of bob and sold for ten shillings, twenty and thirty at a time, fifty and a hundred times a day.

For as one group broke away from the

crowd clutching their precious bundles, others jostled and fought to step forward to get ten shillings for ten shillings and a heap of famous candy free.

Free, gratis and for nothing. More famous words. Run when you hear them.

There was the thin little man who rubbed stains from a worn carpet. He had been rubbing the same stains from the same tattered piece of carpet for thirty years and went on rubbing them for years to follow. And every Sunday the piece of carpet reappeared, miraculously restained, to be restored as miraculously to pristine splendour.

He had a thin piping voice. His English, like his carpet, would never see better days:

"Tex hart (takes out) a fleck from the lapel. Tex hart hoof marks, foot marks, and Carl Marx. Tex hart rains, veins, and stains. Pish, stitch and shitch. Tex hart ott, rott, bloot and snot. Tex hart ink, pink, pitch, candlesgreases and matcheeneries oil.

"Not tree-elefen-tree, two-elefen-tree, vun-elefen-tree . . . "

A slap of the thin hands.

"Troopence!"

The hands met. The goods were for sale.

Ink, pink, pitch, candlesgreases and matcheeneries oil. Immortal phrase. My brother Mark, who was a good mimic, could keep us in fits of laughter retelling this spiel. Can keep us still rolling in the aisles as he brings alively back to mind the market man and his ink, pink, pitch, candlesgreases and matcheeneries oil.

A dapper little man, nattily dressed, sold fountain pens. But no. Never let it be told in the market what you are selling. You are giving it away. To sell the fountain pen he sold nibs. He twisted and turned them into every kind of shape and semblance.

He wrote with the points apart, with the back of the pen, with one point, the other being bent back.

"Looks more like a day's fishing than a day's writing," was his slogan. Yet he managed to write with the nib he had mutilated so severely that his audience wondered how any nib could stand such treatment. And then he cunningly brought the two points together and hey presto! (more famous words. Run when you hear them) the nib was as good as new.

Given away with these nibs was the world-famous pen whose name nobody had ever heard before but now was assumed by all to be world-famous. This pen filled by twisting a screw at its head. Turn to the right to fill. To the left to empty.

What he did not tell them was that every time you wrote five words you would have to turn the screw to keep the ink flowing. I bought one once. The next day my pocket was a mess of ink. My shirt was wet. My body was ink smeared. The entire contents of the pen had seeped away through me and over me.

However, the pen was free. Why look a gift fountain pen in the screw? You paid for the nibs, six of them, and the pen was free with the compliments of its world-famous makers, that nobody had ever heard of, who made their goods in some rat-ridden ruin of a back-alley cellar.

People paid about half a crown for six

nibs worth a penny each and a fountain pen worth threepence, if that.

At the top of The Lane the masked man sold fabulous fortunes for sixpence. In sealed envelopes. Not to be opened till one got home. Or else. The police would pounce on them. On him. Everyone would be in terrible trouble. Fabulous fortunes. He told the story of the famous actor who had stood on London Bridge trying to sell pound notes for a penny and how nobody bought because they were scared. He had been alongside that famous actor. O yes, he had. I believed him . . . then.

Everyone knew the story. True or apocryphal? It didn't matter. All knew it. And this man had been there. And now he was trying to do the same but had to seal the envelopes so that the police could not stop him. Go on. Buy. What can you lose? Sixpence?

You lost sixpence. The envelope contained an out-of-date over-printed German note worth, according to its face valuation, milliards of marks. People even in Germany, where the currency had got so debased that a whole sackful of these was needed to buy one loaf of bread, were papering their rooms with them. Sixpence could have bought a sackful and you would have wanted fourpence change to make the deal legal.

I know. I fell. I bought one once. I fell a lot. I was also a mug. That's how I learned. The bitter way. By experience. People warned me, but I had to find out for myself. That's life, ain't it, as Booba said.

Sarsaparilla. Juicy fruit drinks. All juicy.

Ice cream. Come and buy. Assenheims — they're lovely.

Fruit. The woman who'd learned a few words of Yiddish and called in a Billingsgate accent: "*Veiber, veiber, vehr kohft?*" (Women, women, who's buying?)

Old Barmy — not so old either: no more than a moon-faced twenty-one or two — standing by his barrow of bits and pieces and shouting: "That's all they are . . . that's all they are!"

The same Barmy who, when a Club Camp was proving dull, was invited out to Goring in Sussex, marched from the station to camp with a band of tin kettles and whistles and washboards and paper trumpets leading him, feted, lionized, and then put to sleep in a camp bed, not on the floor like everyone else. And when he was snoring, a pair of kippers that had once known herringed youth, had departed their sea life in old age and that was long long ago, were hung over his broad nose. Barmy who, when he awoke, cried: "Ain't the air fresh here?" and had taken deep gulps of nasalized breath.

Barmy, who if you led him three paces from his haunts, would cry: "Boys . . . I'm lost . . . where am I, boys? . . . Boys, I'm lost!" And the boys would gather round him and buy him a fish and chip supper. Barmy, who was not so Barmy.

Barmy at his stall crying: "That's all they are!"

Fresh cucumbers. Pickled cucumbers. And, believe it or not, pickled apples. Pickled apples. Pickled walnuts, too.

'Addocks, fresh 'addocks.

Glassware . . . lovely glassware. Get your china here. China.

Clothing. Suits to suit you. Perfect fit. Put on a jacket and the salesman's hand went round the back of you pulling in the loose slack so that the front fitted like a glove. Fits you perfect. Could have been made for you. Could have. Was, as he made it.

Shoes. Ladies and gents.

Ladies underwear. I underwear my baby is tonight. And the salesman who did a roaring trade telling the same story every week, fourteen times a day. "No one comes back to me yelling they've been caught. Not like some I could mention not three hundred miles away from here. Like the chap down there who sells Lucky Knickers. You should hear him yellin' '*Lucky knickers, lucky knickers, only three-and-six.*' Girl bought a pair. Nice-looking pair. Nice-looking girl. Took 'em home. Her sister told her she'd been caught. Could-a got 'em at Woolworths for a tanner. Back she runs to the stall. Heaves her way through the crowd. Gets up to the salesman and screams: 'I've, been done! I've been done!' Salesman turns to her, lets her scream her 'I've been done!' turns to the crowd and says: 'You see . . . *lucky* knickers.' Lucky knickers! Lucky knickers! . . . " The laughter sold his sexciting wares. He was a most sexcessful salesman.

And, quietly by his stall, the tubby little thick-set man with a heaped load of spectacles. A very clever man, name of Davis. Had a couple of brilliant children. Boy and girl had both matriculated at thirteen. Went on to Cambridge on scholarships. Father brilliant too. But a drunk. One hell of a drunk. He lived alone, apart from his wife.

Mr. Davis was a frequent visitor to our rooms. He was a good intelligent talker when not in his cups.

At the age of seven I was prescribed spectacles. I went to a place in the City, a big place, official spectacle makers to the L.C.C. and all that. They tested me. Doped my eyes. Later on fitted me with glasses. I came home in tears. I couldn't see a thing. When I tried to say so at the time I was almost thrown out of the shop. A firm with that kind of reputation didn't make mistakes. But I know what they had done. Mixed up my prescription with another boy's. I was blind in those specs and cried all the way home.

Mother took me by the hand and led me across to Mr. Davis. He and his barrow stood there, as mother did, on weekdays too. Mr. Davis took one look at my eyes, one look at the specs, and said to my mother: "The boy's right. They've given him the wrong lenses. Dolts."

With a little instrument that, I suppose, records the focal length of a lens, he went through his tray of lenses, found two, fitted them into my specs and put them on my face.

I saw more clearly than I had done for years. More clearly than I could ever remember having seen. All the little cracks in the paving stones, the cement between the bricks on the walls, the very graining of the bricks. I suddenly saw. It was a delirious feeling.

"How much?"

"Don't be silly, Mrs. Alec. I've got a pair of lenses in exchange, haven't I? Go away and leave me in peace, there's a good woman."

He knew my mother could not afford to pay twice for a pair of spectacle lenses.

And his gruff manner was his way of dealing with the situation.

I wore that same prescription unchanged for thirty years. In fact I wear it still. Not the same lenses, of course, but the same-strength lenses. All those years at seeing through glasses prescribed for me, without drops, without testing, by a street vendor.

When I told my optician about this he wouldn't believe me. A hospital refused to believe it. Impossible, was their verdict. But a Harley Street man was finally convinced, and so interested that he insisted on writing down the story.

"You're a phenomenon," he said.

"Not I," I said. "Mr. Davis."

One night he came into our rooms, sat down heavily on a chair and died. Died right there in our front room. You can imagine the effect on us after we discovered that he had not dropped off to sleep or fainted.

Ought we to call a doctor?

No, counselled my mother. That, she explained, would mean an inquest; and Jews do not believe in inquests unless they are absolutely necessary.

So my brother-in-law Alf, who knew most of the taxi drivers in the East End, ran out to get hold of a pal of his and returned, in about half an hour, to say it was all set. His pal was waiting.

Ben, Mark, Edward and I then got hold of Mr. Davis and began to haul him out of the chair, down the flight of tenement steps, round and through the archway and about fifty yards all told to the waiting taxi on the kerbside in Goolden Street.

Have you ever carried a dead body? It is a frightening weight. I was scared out of my wits. Terrified to be handling a corpse. Shaking with fear lest I dropped my corner of the load.

We got him into the taxi and squeezed in beside him to make room for my mother. Imagine me sitting wedged tight up against a dead body that had to be held in place by my other brothers to prevent it falling forward.

No one saw us, fortunately. God knows what they would have thought.

We got to Mr. Davis's house about half a mile away in Cobb Street, off the Bishopsgate end of Middlesex Street, and then, when the coast was clear, hauled him up the narrow winding stairway behind his front window that was supposed to look like a jeweller's shop, up and up to his small room.

We sat him in a chair, finding great difficulty as I remember in straightening the stiffening limbs. Then we sent for Mrs. Davis who lived about a mile away; brought her round, let her cry herself out, told her she must say she was visiting her husband because she had heard that he was not well (they were separated) and, having got her agreement — anything, short of murder, was permissible if by so doing an inquest could be avoided — we sent for the doctor.

When he came we explained our presence by saying that a distraught Mrs. Davis had sent someone to fetch us, my mother being Mrs. Davis's closest counsellor if not friend. He knew his patient. Knew that Davis had been suffering for a long time of heart trouble; and after an examination pronounced Mr. Davis dead of heart failure. He gave Mrs. Davis a death certificate and we then began to make arrangements for the funeral.

Meantime, Zaida was sent for to watch the body. A dead body must not be left unattended, day or night.

And so Mr. Davis was laid to his rest.

And as I walked through the market when I was getting to be fifteen or sixteen, I always turned to where Mr. Davis had once fitted me with spectacles that suited my eyes so well that the lens prescription was to last me many many years of my life. Today I remember that he succeeded where one of the most famous opticians in the land had failed; and that various ophthalmologists had pronounced his work nothing short of miraculous.

The market was therefore not only an excursion into a dream that came alive with colour but, as the years passed, a remeeting with old memories. There stood the Pen Man; there the Ink, Pink, Carpet Cleaning Man; here the Chocolate King; there the Cockney Fruit Seller spouting Yiddish. Here a face, there a form. Here Mr. Davis, there Barmy.

Yesterday I went through the market

again after nearly thirty years away from it. It was the same. The colour, the sounds, the life, the excitement. Gone were the familiar faces. But in their stead were people and faces strangely reminiscent of those I had known.

There grows the deep where grew the tree, O earth what changes hast thou seen. There where the long street roars hath been the stillness of the central sea. The Tennysonian lines jog the remote fastnesses of memory. The years roll away. I am a boy again.

7

First Knowledge

THERE were many very clever people in Goolden Street — people like Mr. Davis, for instance. But if you said that Broughton Buildings was the abode of whores and bookmakers your generalization would cover at least half of all the tenants of the thousands of flats, and would therefore be as true as it was false. Not that whores were so abundant, though there were plenty of them; but every other door gave access to a bookmaker or a bookmaker's clerk or runner or helper.

The Broughton Buildings women — the honest ones — were often the wives of men engaged in making a living from betting. When times were good they crowded the house with furniture, bought fur coats, jewellery; when the favourites had a long winning run the house grew empty and its clothes cupboards bare.

But the whores never faced this problem. Business was always good. Some of them were married to men who went out to work . . . mostly for bookmakers. One of the most striking was married to a boxer and had borne him two fine children. In fact, I doubt whether the organization that controlled Broughton Buildings would have let their flea-ridden flats to a bachelor or spinster. It was a case of married folks only. So the whores got married.

From the earliest days I knew what an whore was and what she did. So there was no excuse for me when, falling out with a girl I loved, I wrote her a note calling her *an ore*. I mis-spelt deliberately, being cunning enough even then to realize that, if I were caught, I might have a get-out through this deliberate mistake.

Your a little ore, ran my note, *and I don't wont nothing to do with you.*

I pushed the note under her door and forgot it. But her mother, Mrs. Carson, who *was* an whore, took umbrage. Very great umbrage. You could call an whore many things but you dare not call her an whore, nor suggest by refraction that her offspring were at all inclined from the straight and narrow.

Mrs. Carson also guessed that I had written the note and came down to my mother's stall ready to have a fight. But mother was mother. Nobody fought with mother or even lost her temper with Mrs. Alec. Mrs. Alec was a lady. Everyone respected Mrs. Alec. And though Mrs. Carson threatened to go up to my new school (I was just twelve and had only been attending the Grammar School for a short while) she could not have meant it.

Mother was terribly upset and passed over to brother Mark the sad news of my misdemeanour. Mark taxed me with writing the note and I tried to wangle out on the grounds that I had called the young Carson girl a piece of iron. But it didn't work. I could not explain away all my unusual mis-spellings that way, or my laboured attempts at bad grammar.

The final outcome saw me hauled over Mark's knee in a most undignified position for a twelve-year-old, and the very first tanning of my young life ever given me by a member of the family duly administered.

I bore no grudge. I had deserved this. And I knew Mark had to be strict. Some years before he had fallen foul of Mrs. Carson. He had been playing cricket in the playground and, swinging his roughly made bat, had hooked the passing Mrs. Carson below the eye and gashed it.

There was murder. Mrs. Carson began yelling and screaming, giving vent to the foulest string of filthy words anyone ever heard, my mother came running into the yard, Aunt Marfy's hordes of women swept down from their abodes, people came in from the street and the entire playground was a stage on which strutted Mrs. Carson, her eye running blood, declaiming passages beyond the ken of literature; and in a corner of which my brother Mark crouched, comforted only by the protecting arm of mother.

As a tot of about seven or eight I watched these proceedings in horror. But when the police finally arrived — and my mother had a horror which amounted to almost an obsession of getting involved with the law — Mrs. Carson quietened down and the crowd gradually dispersed.

So poor Mark had to tan me then. This was the second contretemps with the magnificent Carson woman.

In future I made no mistakes about writing notes.

One day, when I was getting on for fourteen and knew all about "it", I called at the flat of a friend. He was out. But his mother, a flaming red-haired, squint-eyed woman with the biggest bust you ever saw (and, of course, a pair of very fetching slim legs), called me in and asked me to wait.

I went into the front room and stood uncomfortably about. Mrs. Hyde was dressing apparently, for she had on a loose kimono which barely covered her thighs below, and up top exposed a lot more than was good for me at that tenderly frustrated age.

She caught me ogling her. For she stopped in front of me, and threw her kimono wide open, and said:

"Ain't you never seen 'em before?"

I spluttered. I was horror stricken. I was wishing the floor would open and swallow me up. Mrs. Hyde was not the kind of woman who figured in my dreams. For one thing she had the most out-of-line squint you ever saw and I abhorred squints. For another thing she was old, all of thirty-five or so. And finally, and most horribly, she was an old whore — and I was sickeningly afraid of them — the older they were the viler they grew.

She stood there before me, ridiculously vile, vilely ridiculous.

"'Ow old are yer?"

"Fourteen . . . " I stammered.

"Then you've 'ad the feelin' some time, eh?"

I didn't know how to answer. I was afraid to say *Yes*, ashamed to say *No*.

"Reckon you must 'ave 'ad by now, eh?"

And she chucked me under the chin.

I stood there trembling.

"'Ere," she said kindly, "ain't nothing to be scared of. I won't bite yer . . . jest tryin' to make a man of yer."

And suddenly she had thrown her kimono aside.

She was the first naked woman I had ever seen and she made me feel

79

sick. I couldn't bear to look. I couldn't bear the sight of her stockings, clinging unsymmetrically about legs far too thin for their overblown body. And the sight of her squint leering made me want to vomit.

"Got the feelin' yet?" she asked, and stretched out her hand towards me.

For one awful moment I was paralysed. Then, elbowing past her, I flew for the door, opened it, was through, ran pell-mell down the stairs with her crackling laughter following me and didn't let up till I was safe in my own lavatory closet in our own upstairs flat where no one could grab me.

Thus sex surrounded you in Broughton Buildings. You couldn't escape it. It was part and parcel of everyday living.

But — and here is something for the psychologist to ponder — there was no perversion. Even the whores were respectable and refused to play funny games. It was straight or nothing. My mother used to say they were some of the nicest, kindliest women she had ever met and what a pity it was they had not turned their undoubted talents to other, less rewarding, occupations.

I never met a pansy, a queer or a pervert in all my years at Broughton Buildings. Broughton Buildings was debased perhaps, but it was not depraved; filthy certainly but not slimy.

I knew all about queers, however. You can't grow up in that sort of place, however ignorant you may be, to discover gaps in your sexual education.

Jimmy (born Judah) Kern (born Cohen) was a very good actor as a child, took part in school plays, gained London Federation of Boys' Clubs award for individual recitations of dramatic art.

Jimmy topped the school in his last year for his work and performances in class and on stage. He went out into the world of the theatre with hopes brimming high.

He was tall, fair, very good to look on. He bore himself proudly. Long years of elocution had given him a cultured, modulated, forward-thrown voice. His eyes were brown, his body was slim and everyone said he would be a film star.

He was then a close friend of brother Mark's and came back many evenings each week to report on his progress. I was not supposed to listen — I was at my books and supposedly swotting — but I caught all the whispering that went on.

Jimmy was having some disturbing experiences.

To him, brought up in the call-a-spade-a-spade, use-a-spade-as-a-spade atmosphere of Broughton Buildings, these were so repulsive that at first he couldn't believe they were genuine and then, when he knew they were, couldn't bear to hear. Twice he had punched a would-be seducer on the point of the chin.

As the months went by and Jimmy couldn't get fixed up, he grew embittered and angry. Two of his drama school colleagues earned themselves West End appearances on the stage. These two were so much Jimmy's inferior in talent and ability that it made him writhe to learn of their success. Jimmy got nowhere fast.

After a year he went into tailoring. The theatre lost a potential star, but Broughton Buildings gained a notable triumph for its own naturally unclean, uncleanly natural way of life.

8

Zaida

FROM perversion to pertinacity. From faithlessness to faith. To get a true picture of the East End as it was then, it is necessary to recall that there were villains, but there were heroes, too.

My boyhood hero was my grandfather.

Zaida was a chunky, strong man with a magnificent grey-black beard, a face that reminded one of an eagle or a red Indian chieftain. Yet he had the most wonderful sense of humour a man ever had for all his stern countenance. You saw it in his eyes, twinkling blue, alight with good-natured fun.

He was fanatically devout. On Friday evenings he went off to synagogue to usher in the Sabbath. When we were young, my brothers and I went with him. We respected him and we did it to please him.

After the service we'd sit down at home to a table spread with a white cloth, the candles gleaming, a feeling of unusualness around. Friday evenings were different — holier, brighter, gayer, devouter, different — from other days. Not till they were grown-up men and women did any of the family dare miss the Friday night gathering at home.

To greet the Sabbath Zaida would stand up and, with the glass of wine in his hand, recite the Sabbath prayer and bless us. O the unforgettable togetherness of those candle-lit Sabbath evenings . . . O the ties of love that bound us, the oneness that held us close . . . O the dead Friday evenings and the dead dear souls of my youth.

He spent most of Saturday at the synagogue. He spent most of the holy Fast days and Festivities in the synagogue. Rab Yitzchak — Mr. Isaac (his first name) — was a devout and much admired member of a small back-street congregation.

On the eve of Yom Kippur, the Day of Atonement, he would go off to the synagogue after a light meal my Booba prepared for him, stand in his stockinged feet all night before the altar praying, take part in prayers and fasting the following day, come home at night, eat sparingly and go to bed. While others, even the rabbi, slept away at least six or seven hours of the twenty-four-hour Fast, Zaida fasted awake and on his feet for a full twenty-five hours from sundown on the eve of Atonement to sunset the following day. From the blowing of the Shofar, the ram's horn, which initiates the solemn occasion, to the single blast on the Shofar that ends it.

He did it because he believed. He believed with a perfect faith. He believed in one God, one law, one element to which the whole creation moves. Everything was the will of the God. He never grumbled and he never worked and everyone loved him. Mother used to get him to keep an occasional eye on the stall; but he was a pretty bad business man and often sold articles for far less than mother had paid to buy them.

His wants were few. He did not need money, never asked for it. A little tobacco for his pipe, a bed to sleep in — no, a place to sleep in, a place, that's all — the synagogue . . . and he was happy. He adored his grandchildren and they worshipped him. He quarrelled incessantly with Booba, his wife, talked to my mother as though she were still his teenage daughter — yet listened respectfully to her when she had cause to upbraid him — and spoilt the children with his grand sense of fun. Apart from his faith Zaida took little else seriously.

A man of immense physical strength, he was as gentle as a babe with all. He could sit my younger sister Lily on the palm of his outstretched hand and then me on the other and balance our weights. He could lift up the four corner poles of the stall when they were wrapped in wet tarpaulin and bear them upon his shoulders. It normally took two of us to lift one sodden tarpaulin-wrapped pole.

He never mastered more than a few words of English. Yiddish was his language. That's how we all learned to speak it. Booba and Zaida spoke nothing else. We grew up with Yiddish. It led to some awkward situations. When my sister Lily had her bead necklace broken she told the class teacher that young Johnny Cohen had shit out all her beads. Everyone was horrified. But Lily was merely using the Yiddish expression for "to spill", the bastardized German of "auschitten", which we all used in speaking as "shit out".

Once Zaida was trundling me on the barrow back to the shed where it was housed overnight. Goolden Street was being repaired and was up; so we went through Middlesex Street, the Lane itself.

In those days the number 78 'bus used to run through Middlesex Street on weekdays — nothing could have got through there on a Sunday, not even a foot-propelled toy scooter.

Zaida's barrow impeded a hurrying 'bus. The driver tootled. There was nowhere for Zaida to veer to, so he stayed on course. The road was narrow and there were 'buses coming against him in the other direction.

The driver swore.

Zaida kept on.

"Get out of the bleedin' way!" roared the 'bus driver.

Zaida went on.

The 'bus driver, angered, stopped his 'bus, climbed down, ran ahead of it and seized Zaida's arm.

He let loose a torrent of abuse. Now although Zaida hadn't much English he had, like all foreigners, quickly mastered the swear words. And he was also a very good mimic.

So when the driver swore at him, he repeated the driver's words in the driver's own language. Bystanders laughed. The driver grew madder and madder.

He began to get personal. "Mucking Jew bastard!"

"You, mucking bastard!" said Zaida.

"I'll knock your mucking block off!"

"You, mucking block off!"

"Get out of the bleedin' way you shitbag!"

"You, shitbag!"

At which the driver lost control immediately and took a mighty swipe at my grandfather. Zaida sidestepped nimbly, brought his arm round from his ear in a wide sweeping gesture — his famous Russian punch — and knocked the driver flat into the middle of the dung heaps on the road.

People ran to the aid of the semi-conscious driver who was still wondering what had hit him. Zaida put me back on the barrow and trundled on unmolested.

During the Beaver Craze when you scored points for every beard you saw, Zaida came in for a good deal of good-natured banter. If a short goatee was a one-er and a French taz a two-er, then Zaida's beard was a ten-er. It was worth every Beaver fan's notice.

He stood the chaff and the catcalls and the finger pointing for many a week without turning a grey hair. Then one day two louty young fellows went flying by on a horse-driven van and yelled "Beaver!" high and clear.

My grandfather was after them in a trice. He outsped the galloping horses, got abreast of the van, pulled it up with a flying leap, went up and into it in one bound and with one mighty Russian punch swept them both flying on to the road. Their faces, as they wiped the blood from them and took their seats again in the van, were a study. How did this bearded ancient ever have the legs to catch them and the strength to knock them both from their perches?

Of course the beard and the white hairs were misleading. Zaida was at this time about sixty, no more, as fit and agile, nimble and healthy as anyone half his age, and just about twice as strong.

On another occasion a tram driver in Commercial Street ignored his waving arm at the stop and sailed by. Some of them were swines. When they saw elderly Jewish men and women waiting they deliberately put on speed to pass them.

Two hundred and fifty yards up the road the tram had to stop at the junction of Commercial Street with Aldgate High Street and Commercial Road.

Zaida knew this and began to chase.

He caught the tram before it could move off again and stood in the centre rail right in front of it so that it could not proceed and inquired of the tram driver:

"Vy you no stop?"

The tram driver's answer to this was short and sweet.

"Bollocks!" he said.

Zaida addressed himself to the

passengers who crowded the tram's lower and upper decks.

Sweeping his arm in their direction he roared: "Bollocks — I got vitnesses for bollocks . . . I got vitnesses for bollocks!" and then, under the impression that witnesses were sufficient to justify any course he took, leaned up and over the tram, seized the driver by his coat lapels, lifted him high and over the platform and held him up in the air for all to see.

Then he put him down gently on the floor and said gently: "Next time you stop, no?"

Jewish dead must be watched during the night. Zaida watched the dead. He was a qualified "Watcher". He also watched the making of Passover biscuits and cakes under jurisdiction, many times removed, of the Chief Rabbi.

For these tasks he was paid; and as this was the only money he ever earned he would bring it home delightedly and plonk it down into my mother's hand and say with pride: "Na", here you are, as if to prove that he, too, could make money as well as and as easily as the next man.

He was also a film star. A company, looking for bearded men to play a funeral scene, fastened on to my grandfather and paid him a guinea a day as an extra. This was riches indeed.

Zaida, the most impressive looking of all the men they recruited, led a funeral cortège. Zaida was the leading pall bearer. They were told to chant under their breaths, for although this was the pre-talkie era the producers wanted realism.

And Zaida led them into a little song which all the hundred or so bearded extras took up and they marched slowly and sang softly to Zaida's bidding. It was most impressive. The producer was so touched he upped Zaida's pay to thirty bob a day and told him the scene had been most moving.

The song they chanted was not in Hebrew at all, certainly not in prayer Hebrew, but a rather lewd ballad in Yiddish about the town whore.

For another scene Zaida was singled out to cry dramatically over the coffin of a Roman emperor. They dressed him in a toga and asked him to go up there and make gestures and cry out anything aloud.

He bestrode the tomb like a Colossus and cried dramatically in Yiddish: "So die all uncircumcized!"

He was a wow.

Loved by old and young, my Zaida went through this life believing in God, adoring children and smiling at people. To me he was father and God together. My father had died when I was three and Zaida was the greatest man on earth for me.

He loved me, too. I was the bright one, the scholar, the boy destined to be a rabbi. Even in those days nothing was further from my thoughts; but to please him I went to the *Yeshiva* (the Hebrew High School) in the evenings and on Sundays, and learned to discourse on the Bible and understand the scholarly arguments about the text.

This was much further than most Jewish boys went. They merely attended *Cheder* or *Talmud Torah* classes, the equivalent of lower-grade secular schools, learned a little Hebrew, could translate portions of the Bible and the Prayer Book and were then *Barmitzvah* (confirmed). After this solemn ceremony they left *Cheder* at the age of thirteen and never bothered to learn any more Hebrew as long as they lived.

Brighter pupils, and the few who were willing to do so, or were compelled by parents to do so, went on to the *Yeshiva* to study the Bible, write Hebrew, learn grammar and become true Hebrew scholars.

I was most unwilling to spend my leisure hours doing this; but for Zaida's sake I did. Not out of fear — in all his life he never lifted a finger to me or said an angry word to me — but out of respect.

He was getting on for eighty and still as strong as an ox when, crossing Commercial Street to get to his synagogue, his stick caught in the centre rail of the tramline and a tram came along and knocked him down. It was as if the trams had taken vengeance on him for daring to assault one of their drivers years before.

He died without regaining consciousness. At the inquest they told us, hoping to comfort us maybe but succeeding only in adding to our anguish, that he had the heart, lungs and physique of a man of thirty.

And that was the end of Zaida.

For days afterwards I was lost. I wanted the traffic to stop and people to halt and all London to stand still and honour the most wonderful man who had ever lived.

I could not cry. But somewhere inside me the agony welled and all my inner being was torn apart. I did not go to college lectures. Did not eat. Just wandered about London, lost and despairing. Zaida, my Zaida was dead. The world had come to an end.

O that gentle smile and that stern faith. That strong body and that delicate sense of humour. That fierce love for his brood and his hatred of unfairness. O my grandfather. Zaida, I weep for you . . . still, in the cold chill of morning, still, in the sad slow hours of night I wake and weep.

Somewhere in his heaven the trumpets blazed him a welcome and a vast army rose to greet this godlike man, this man of God who never in all his life did a wicked thing.

No, not a heaven, but a Valhalla. For he was of the breed of which those Vikings of old were made. And I can see him there, supping his wine, as he loved to sup it, and then suddenly stopping and winking and saying: "I'll get myself some fresh air." Even in his love of wine he was strong and determined and knew when to stop. Knew? Knows! For Zaida can never be dead. He was too much alive, too much a part of life, too content with living and loving and giving to know blankness, immobility, nothing.

He believed in life. He believed in God. He believed his every act was pre-ordained and that from all the chaos of misfortune the inexorable event built itself up to welcome man to Paradise. His living was a small part of that one far-off divine event to which the whole creation moves.

O Zaida, how you haunt me with your large fawnlike eyes and your smile like a contented child at its mother's breast and your devotion to your family, your faith, to man, to God. O there is no longer any beauty in the forest, no whisper in the breeze, no violet on the far hills. O dead and gone and alive . . . only in my memory? Only in my memory!

9

Booba

OUT of the rain falling and the wild stars winking and the wind tearing itself apart in agony and the earth groaning . . . out of sorrow and sadness and travail my grandmother was born.

She was born to work and work and suffer and suffer and there was no respite for her all the days of her life.

Booba was old. Always old. When I first grew aware of her, my second mother, she was bent and wispy-haired and witch-like. She was never young and she never got to looking any older.

From the day she was brought to London by her daughter, my mother, she slaved for her brood. She it was who prepared the meals and did the cleaning, and scrubbed and polished and made the house home.

She rarely left the house. And in all the

time we lived in Broughton Buildings I never remember her leaving her basement flat to come up to our first-floor flat. The earth was her habitation and there she stayed.

As she slept the rats ran across her and she never complained, merely told us about them in her dry, matter-of-fact voice.

Unlike Zaida she had no sense of humour. She was too intense. I never saw her sit down and relax. She couldn't read — except a bit of Prayer Book Hebrew — and she never could understand the ways of the strange city in which she found herself.

But she never complained. This was her lot. This her portion in life. This was what God had chosen her to do on earth.

Edward, my eldest brother, was her favourite. He was the first-born. The all-important. And he it was who, because he was the first one out of school and into work, brought her sweets and chocolates and little gifts which she adored.

But her love for us all was still big enough even when she gave so much to

Edward. She watched us, sewed our torn garments, tended us when sick.

Occasionally she would potter out to the shops around the corner and buy a few groceries. Other than this she never went out. In all her life at Broughton Buildings she never left London, never saw the sea she had once crossed in the hold of a cargo boat sailing between Danzig and London Docks.

Mother was her only child. Booba had lost others in childbirth. The son my Zaida would have adored was never born. So the devotion of both was transferred to their grandchildren, to us. Zaida's devotion was obvious, joyful, extrovert, exultant. Booba's was proud and deep and as abiding as eternity.

She preferred the boys to the girls. Girls, she said, were *kleine pisherkies*, little bed-wetters, but a boy was strength and joy.

Boys were also less expensive, didn't spend their money on fripperies, were more cognisant of the home's needs and brought money into the house instead of taking it out. It was a realistic view. For my sisters, bless their hearts, were always a drain on the family exchequer while my brothers, once they were working, kept the house going.

In turn Edward was first the father of the family, and then Mark. They took over the duties of being the breadwinner and bore the burden nobly many years.

Ben and I were luckier. We were the younger sons, I the youngest, and by the time we were earning money the family was on its feet at last.

Zaida and Booba always looked to the boys to provide a *Kuddish* for them. When a Jew dies his nearest male relative says a prayer for him each day for a year in the synagogue and ever afterwards on holy days and each *Yahrzeit*, the anniversary of the death.

We were to be the *Kuddishim*, the prayer-reciters, for Booba and Zaida. They fervently believed that these prayers, diligently recited, would speed them to Paradise. Hence another reason for preferring boys to girls. Girls could not say *Kuddish*, were not allowed to by religious law.

There are not many stories to tell about my Booba. Her life was too quiet, too unexciting to make reading. She once had bad ulcers on her legs and these my mother tended and cured without calling the doctor. They never recurred, so mother, who had a little knowledge of medicine, having started to become a doctor before she switched to Russian schoolteaching, did a good job.

Mother used to tell us that Jewish medical students were allowed to qualify only by strict quota. The Czar's régime, in common with other dictatorial régimes, did not like Jews. Mother saw that her chances of making the grade were almost hopeless — a woman doctor and Jewish at that. It would never be allowed. So she became a village schoolmistress.

But when Booba began to complain of clouded vision, mother immediately diagnosed cataract. To put Booba into hospital was unthinkable. No Jews of that generation ever left home, even to go to hospital. In such strange surroundings Booba would have been lost.

So, remembering some old village remedy, or calling upon her forgotten medical knowledge, mother took some very fine grains of sugar and blew them into Booba's eye.

Booba began to cry with pain. She clasped her hands to her eyes and rocked backwards and forwards in grief. We stood there horrified. What had mother done?

For a long time, perhaps half an hour, we stood there helpless as Booba, who was not one to complain of pain, almost tore herself apart in agony.

And then, slowly, the pain subsided, the eye cleared and Booba could see. She was never again troubled with cataract or any other ophthalmological ailment. Till the end of her days she never wore glasses and could sew the tiniest stitches without artificial aid.

Was it a remedy for cataract, this blowing of fine sugar grains into the eye? I do not know. Perhaps it wasn't cataract at all, though it appeared to be from Booba's description of the film over her eye that prevented her seeing. However, the remedy worked. I can bear witness to that. And an eye which had been troublesome for months was restored to normal with a single drastic treatment. Is

103

there a doctor in the house? Well, what do you think, brother?

Booba's command of English was even less than Zaida's. He had the advantage of being a mimic. She didn't even mix with people and her opportunities for learning were limited.

Names bothered her. She could never get them right. And her attempts to repeat a name always sent us into fits of laughter. Hearing us laugh, Booba wouldn't turn a hair. Not a smile appeared on those wrinkled cheeks. But there was never any trace of anger, either. She mispronounced names so often that I am certain she liked to hear us laugh and just as certain that she could never have pronounced them any other way.

Mrs. Dickens became, in Booba's language, "Mrs. Pickle". Mrs. Rowbotham, "Mrs. Ruffbottom". Mr. Smokolvitch, "Mr. Shmokstitch". Her linguistic activities extended to everyday things. Chloride of lime, always used in washing, became "Kloddovvalibe". Smoked haddock, "Smokkannock". Tangerines, "Change-a-greens".

But perhaps Booba's funniest was in

calling the highly respected Sir Basil Henriques, who ran the clubs we used to attend, "Mister Hendricks".

Always frail, always tired-looking, Booba none-the-less had tremendous reserves of energy. She was first up, preparing the morning meal; last to bed, insisting on waiting up until we were all home, often sitting up till two or three in the morning to see us safely back, as we grew older, from the dances or parties or dates we were enjoying.

Such a patient woman she was. So undemanding. Rightly or wrongly — and maybe wrongly — my mother put her in charge of the house. My mother could never be bothered with domestic chores — these were for the stupid and the ignorant — and it was left to Booba to clean up and cook and scrub and patch the clothes. My mother considered these jobs beneath her. So Booba became the unpaid servant who uncomplainingly gave up her years of living to further ours. She never once protested. I am convinced she thought it was her destiny, her right, and did not question it. But I question it now. Such pathetic resignation should never have been allowed. Booba deserved better things than were ever given her, than she ever knew.

She just grew older and older and feebler and feebler and one day she took to her bed and just faded away into a sleep as undemonstrative as the life she had lived.

O Booba. Exile in a strange land, stranger in a forbidding street. Four walls her masters. They constrained her and sustained her. She walked upon village roads in Poland and they led straight to Broughton Buildings and rats. She stooped because the skies hung low. She was bent because the many flats above her weighed on her back.

Was she ever a child? Did she ever skip and romp and run and play? Weave flowers in her hair? Know the surging joy of spring? Dance with the sheer exuberance of being born?

Always old, always bent, always wrinkled; feeble, frail and quiet, so quiet; patiently she lived and patiently patiently she died.

She forever threatened to outlive Zaida and she did. But the heaven she believed in will never solve her problem, for the last person she would want to meet there in a foreverness of living would be Zaida. Here were two opposites, the extrovert and the introvert, the exultantly faithful and the intensely zealous who found togetherness only in a mutual love for their brood.

So wait for us all, dear Zaida, darling Booba, to reunite you both in the everlasting.

10

Relatives and Friends

MY brother Edward "fathered" me, *loco parentis*. He was a very good footballer, a well-known and very clever amateur outside-left. And he was the inspiration behind our fondness for games. We all excelled at sport, were fast runners, agile athletes, ambidextrous two-footed flanneled fools and muddied oafs.

He took me to see soccer matches. We went to Wembley. We saw the wonderful Wembley Wizards.

Zaida used to laugh at us. "Footbollick" he would say: "grown mens running around like meshuga, med. Footbollick. Nothing with nothing."

But we played and we watched and we talked loudly and longly about our favourite teams and players.

Then, as Edward got himself married and moved out, Mark became my leader and guide. His tastes were a little more catholic. He took me to the cinema often, the theatre occasionally, "up West" to Lyons Corner House for Friday afternoon teas. Of all my brothers he had the greatest influence in moulding my life. He had a fine, quick brain; a wide range of interests; a wonderful knack of remembering good stories and of being able to recapture popular music he had heard only once. And he was a fine character, sincere, solidly right in his approach to difficult problems, not given to panic or hasty judgement; discerning, tolerant, understanding. Between us there was a kinship which time strengthened.

But Ben I was closest to. He was but two years my senior and we were boys together.

We went to *Cheder* together. There we were taught Hebrew and eventually found ourselves sitting together in the top class.

Hebrew classes were a joke. An imposition, a detention, a source of resentment, but a joke. If we had to go there we could make the most of the evenings. That was the general attitude.

Boys in those days regarded *Cheder* as a necessary evil where it was proper to do all the silly things one dare not do at school.

Discipline had to be strict or there would have been nightly riots. The weak teachers went through it far worse than any weak teacher at school ever did.

Our teacher in the top class was a short roly-poly man with narrow pig's eyes and a heavy beard down to his swollen middle. He growled and he scowled and the boys were terrified of him.

Bully, they called him. *Old Bully-boy*. His favourite form of torture was the *bully-pinch*, a twisting of the flesh on your behind. It made you yelp and it left a mark.

Behind him at his desk against which he leaned during lesson time, *Bully* kept a bottle of water. When his throat grew dry he would turn round, take a swig of liquid, put the bottle down and go on with the lesson.

One day my brother Ben had his vision clouded by eye drops. Poor Ben was always having eye trouble. An avid reader, he used to sit in the front row of the cinema and read his Buffalo Bill and his Sexton Blake, or sit up half the night reading tiny print under his bedclothes by the light of a torch. No wonder his spectacle lenses were pebble thick.

On this evening he had once again had drops put into his eyes and he couldn't see clearly. He told *Bully*. Though it took some time to sink in to the thick skull, *Bully* finally understood what Ben was trying to say.

He motioned Ben with his fat stubby fingers to sit behind him, facing the class, at the big desk.

After a time Ben grew bored. From his pockets he fished a nigroid, a small dark brown pellet we used to buy in tins. We used to suck these pellets when our throats were dry.

Ben played with this nigroid for a while. Then, to my horror, he dropped it into *Bully's* bottle of water. This was the sort of lemonade bottle that used to be made with a glass marble in the neck to prevent the liquid contents gushing out. The pellet stuck on the marble. Gingerly, Ben shook the bottle.

Bully turned round in a flash. The look

of innocence on Ben's cherubic face had to be seen to be believed. Out of his misted eyes he looked through *Bully* at the dark brown wall ahead. Such acting would have convinced anyone.

Seeing nothing wrong, *Bully* turned back and went on with the lesson. Fascinated, I watched as the water turned dark brown, liquorice-coloured.

Came the time for *Bully's* drink. He whipped round, seized the bottle, held it to his overfull, over-red lips and let the dirty brown liquid trickle into his mouth. It went glub-glub-glub. The glass marble and *Bully's* adam's apple bobbed up and down, up and down, in liquifactory concert.

Suddenly *Bully* put the bottle down. He had noticed or tasted something amiss. He glared malevolently at Ben. The height of innocence gazed back at him. *Bully* and Bubbles. Malaise and Millais.

I waited for the thick heavy hand to wipe itself around Ben's face. I felt sorry for Ben and what was to come to him.

But *Bully* suddenly whipped round again, darted between the aisles of desks, seized hold of Polliver, the bad boy of the class, by the scruff of the neck, hauled him kicking and protesting to the top of the stairs and then, shaking him like a rat, threw him down the whole flight.

During break we rushed out into the street to find Polly. He was not to be seen. Had he been hurt? Poor Ben was terribly anxious.

But next night Polly was back in his seat again, *Bully* was twisting the buttocks of those who spoke, Ben was in his seat next to mine and the world went on as usual.

I remember the occasion when Ben was picked to play for the school cricket team. He was a very stylish bat but he could not score runs and I watched as he struggled for many overs before being bowled for a duck. However, he had held his end up and had not let me down.

But when his turn to field came, every catch seemed to move his way. And even as he got under it and set himself for it I knew he could not really see the ball. He could not see anything beyond six inches from his nose.

And as Ben dropped a succession of

catches I wished the earth would swallow me up. How he felt I never knew, for we never referred to the subject. Ben did not play cricket again for the school. He took up gymnastics and Ju Jitsu . . . *Gentile Jitsu*, as we happily called it, practising holds with Jerry Short (of whom I shall tell later).

At soccer, however, Ben made the grade at centre-forward and scored regularly. This gave me great joy. I basked in his reflected glory.

Together we went on holiday to Brighton. Together we played in the playground. We shared the same bed, the same family jokes, the same friends. We were pals.

He was Booba's second favourite, after Edward. She made her likes quite clear. As a child he had needed a lot of nursing and Booba had seen him through one bronchitic winter after another. He was hers. And none of us felt any jealousy over it.

Then once, after a bout of sickness, he went away to convalescent home for a month, and I moped and sought for him all through a succession of hot, endless

114

days. When he finally came home I cried with relief.

After that he was different. He had outgrown me. He was bigger and tougher than he'd ever been before. He'd found new interests. He left school and went out to work.

The schoolboy David and Jonathan link had been broken. Now we were just good friends.

Left alone, I began to seek my own friends and made friends with three boys who were to be my close associates for the next six or seven years.

There was Shorty, so called because of his lack of inches. Short, tubby, laughing-eyed, Shorty always engaged me in bitter struggle for the position of top boy. We went through school deadly rivals yet close friends.

His mother was also a widow. But their stall in Brick Lane did much better business than my mother's in Goolden Street. They sold pots and pans. Shorty's mother and brothers all helped in the family business. Compared with us they were very wealthy.

Harry was a tall thin boy, frailer even

than I was. His mother was another widow. Harry's father and six of his father's brothers had died of T.B. and the inheritance had stamped itself on Harry's narrow shoulders and concave chest.

He was the poorest of us all. Mother, of course, took pity on him and many a meal did he eat with us. Although he was no fool he did not do very well at school work. Then, just before his matriculation, he fell sick of the same illness that had played havoc with his family.

The disease brought out in him hidden depths of brilliance as if it had set fire to long-smouldering genius. Returning to school after a long session in the sanatorium, he achieved distinction in every subject he took, went on to shatter school educational records, to take a degree in both Arts and Science, both with first-class honours, and to wind up as one of the most brilliant writers in Fleet Street.

Then there was Hyman my closest friend.

He was perhaps the most comfortable, in matters of money and background, of us all. His mother had a little grocery shop near Spitalfields. His father was still alive and went out to work until the shop was doing such good business that he could afford to stay at home and help his wife run it.

His mother was English born, his father foreign. This gave Hyman a rather superior air of being somewhat better bred.

He was a tall, gangling, good-looking boy. He had a mass of fair curly hair, a pleasant smile, an easy manner. He was intelligent, too; but never really shone at school work.

Good at games, a good athlete, ready witted, well dressed in made to measure suits, Hyman fancied himself as the leader of our little group though all would have disputed any one particular person's claims to leadership.

My mother liked him. My sisters adored him. My brothers quite accepted him. He ate in my house and I ate in his, comparing the difference, when I did so, between his neat little house with its tidy furniture and clean walls and our own hovel-like habitation.

Hyman and I were thick as thieves. We were always together. We took holidays together and he made the dates for the girls we got to know together.

But always at school I was way ahead of him. And though I never dreamed it, this rankled him.

When we had taken matric together we went off on holiday to Ramsgate.

I had not worked very hard. To me there had never been any necessity to swot. Exams were meant to be taken in one's stride. But I did not do as well as I had confidently expected. My pride in myself took a sharp blow.

Hyman, who had worked furiously, sitting up half the night and slaving away weekends, never sparing himself to master the set subjects, won two distinctions. For him this was triumph. For me, a similar result was comparative failure.

One night in our Ramsgate room he suddenly turned to me and said: "You know I'm cleverer than you, don't you? Come on now, confess it . . . I *am* cleverer than you, aren't I?" I was lost for a reply.

118

Our holiday petered out. And after that Hyman and I stopped seeing one another. We went separate ways. He took up accountancy and was soon earning money. Even if something had not come between us I would have been unable to keep pace with the free-spending set he went around with.

To Harry, who became something of a genius in his late teens, I would gladly have given way. But to Hyman, the fair, good-natured, superior, charming Hyman — never.

11

Down the Airy

ONE thing that bound Hyman and me together — and Shorty too — was our fanatical fondness for football.

As a youngster I was always playing football. If there were no boys around, I played alone, dribbling and shooting, catching the rebound off a wall and passing to myself. If there was no ball available we made one of paper and string and kicked that around. We played with footballs, tennis balls, coloured balls, little tiny balls, even with glass pebbles. Anything that resembled a ball, however vaguely, was game enough for a game.

The rivalry that existed between the three playgrounds, the Top Arch, Middle Arch and Bottom Arch, was fierce and furious. Games were played in the Bottom Arch because it had the largest playground. Usually, just when the game was most exciting, a shout would go up — "Look out, it's Gammylegs!" And everyone would disperse just as Mr. Harris, the caretaker, came hobbling into the field of vision.

He was the bane of our life was Gammylegs. He hobbled into view just when games were at their most enjoyable and broke them up. Playing ball games, cycling too, were forbidden inside the playgrounds. And he seemed to sense the time when matches took place. I never knew one that finished at the *Six wins* or *Ten wins* scheduled point of termination.

We didn't play by the hour. We played to a total. Sometimes a game would drag on interminably. Players would leave to go home. Others would drift in. And then, just when victory loomed close for one side or the other — presto! in hobbled Gammylegs shouting fire and breathing threats.

We grew agile, too, at recovering our balls from perilous perches on the glass roof of the factories that were about eight feet from the ground above the concrete wall that bounded the far sides of the playgrounds.

Then there were the areas. The playgrounds were onion shaped. The narrow opening from the Goolden Street end was through the Arch. You came into an elliptical playground, surrounded by left and right arcs of huge tenements and, facing, the concrete wall of the Middlesex Street factories.

All around were the areas, about six feet below ground, about ten to twelve feet wide. They were fenced by closely set iron railings at least five feet high.

When a ball went into the area — the "airy" as we called it — we had to climb the railings and dive down to rescue it.

When I think now of the turns I made with my heels wedged between sharp pointed rails about three inches apart and the drops and lifts I went through each day to retrieve lost balls, I marvel at my agility.

In years of retrieving lost balls and watching other kids go for their prizes, I never saw anything remotely resembling an accident. We were like cats. Sure-footed and confident of our way.

I did more retrieving than most. When my long holidays took me, lonely and companionless, into deserted playgrounds I began to hit a tennis ball against the wall with an old racket. I got so good that I could pick my spots, forehand or backhand, and was volleying with force and precision before I even knew how tennis was played.

For some time, as I grew up, I was ball boy to my brothers Edward and Mark when they went to play tennis in Victoria Park every Friday afternoon. One day I prevailed upon them to let me play. They did laughingly. I beat them both, quite easily. My years of practice against the factory walls paid off.

I was playing for a club one day in Victoria Park when a stranger approached me and asked me whether I got regular coaching and, if I did not, whether I would be willing to call at an address in the West End where a Youth Council encouraged youngsters to become proficient at tennis.

I told the man it was impossible. I told him I was too busy getting through my school exams — I was about fifteen then. The real truth was that I was not very interested. Football was my game.

The playgrounds were the hunting grounds of those kids whose tenements faced or were nearest to the asphalted spaces.

There were nearly always some children about. The girls with a skipping rope:

One, two, three, O'Leary,
My ball's down the airy,
Pick it up and give it to Mary
On a Sunday morning.

The boys with the inevitable ball and only occasionally with tops or ropes. Diabolo, yes. We were expert at manipulating the diabolo and, on Sundays, would find a place in Goolden Street where, surrounded by crowds drifting in and out of the Market, we threw high, higher, still higher, throwing and catching the diabolo with a facility born of vast experience. And the crowds would throw us pennies.

Occasionally we would divide into gangs and play hunting and chasing games. The running party, given a few minutes start, would lay tracks, chalk signs mostly, for the pursuing party to follow.

And off we'd go, into the quietness of the City on Sundays or Saturday evenings, far along Leadenhall Street and down all the little twisted streets and back through the side turnings of slumbering Bishopsgate and so home as night fell.

My friend of those days, Jackie Pruse, and I played a secret hand of saving farthings. We found a place in a quiet square off Bishopsgate, Devonshire Square, I think it was, and there, down in the basement yard, just by the side of the iron stairway, we found a loose brick in one of the walls and there we placed all our farthings.

The idea was that at some time in the future we could pretend to stumble on this ancient hoard of buried treasure.

For many months we went on saving farthings and then, for some reason, we stopped playing that game.

Just before we left Broughton Buildings, I, being then a grown youth of sixteen or seventeen, was passing through this sleepy square one summer's evening when I suddenly remembered our secret cache.

I went down the stairs leading to the basement area, felt for the stone and, removing it, was surprised, delighted and, I must confess, a little nostalgic even then, to find the farthings still there. There must have been about fifty, all told, but what memories they evoked. Each coin brought its dream walking, each chink echoed a boyhood escapade.

I stood there, alone in that little space in that quiet square on a summer's evening as the twilight surrounded me and the shadows slowly folded me to them.

And then, as night came on to sadden and depress me, I put the brick back and went silently, sadly away. There, for the first time, I knew that I had stopped being a boy. Gone, like my youth, were the days that had swallowed me into their never-ending round of activity. Gone, like the day that had just closed, never again to be.

For all I know the hoard of farthings is still there.

Treat them lightly if you find them. They are precious dreams of gallant boyhood adventures, symbols of a dear departed era. They are not coins but glimpses of the past, of the days when I was a boy and all the world was wide.

12

Grammar School

I WENT from the Jews' Free School to the Davenant Foundation School in the Whitechapel Road. It was at that time called the Whitechapel Foundation School, but old boys protested that the name was a bar to progress and, soon after I joined the school, it became known after its founder, Sir Ralph Davenant — or was it Sir William?

Shorty, Hyman, a dark-faced lithe lad called Bernie and I all gained scholarships together and started our life at Davenant in the same form on the same day.

Despite its name, the Whitechapel Foundation School had a glorious tradition of scholarship. Its examination results were outstanding. And its figures for passes in the then Matriculation and Higher Schools examinations of London University were nearly twenty per cent

128

above the average for the rest of the country.

From it came a string of doctors, most of them moving across the road to the London Hospital, the largest in the world at that time. Teachers were produced by the score. Lawyers by the dozen. The school's record of men who had achieved distinction, without wealth or position to give them a prod, was unique.

The staff was a body of devoted men; they must have found their job worth while. For here was gathered a collection of brains, talent and ability that needed but the minimum encouragement to flower into brilliance.

Right at the beginning I found in the English master, Mr. Evans, Gobby Evans as we called him, a kindred soul. He loved his subject passionately and managed to impart his adoration for it to most of us.

I revelled in the poetry he led us to appreciate; in the prose he taught us to understand. I lapped up every word of his teaching and he, sensing my love of words and phrases and verbal music, encouraged me and guided me.

There came a time when I was writing an essay every evening for Mr. Evans and looking forward to the daily voluntary task with as much excitement as most boys of that age look forward to respite from homework. I had free choice of subject and, as I filled exercise book after book with my scribblings, the bonds between Mr. Evans and myself strengthened.

In school itself I was happy. Out of school there were my friends, the unchanging regulars, Shorty, Hyman, Harry and others who from time to time were gathered into our quartet.

Such a one was the sallow dark-faced boy who had won his scholarship when we did. Bernie was bright. Good at games, good at his work, he was popular with boys and teachers.

But, at the age of fourteen, his father died and he had to leave. I forgot all about Bernie until I saw him soon after the war. I ran across him in Staines by the river and the recognition was mutual.

The difference between us was vast. Although we had come from similar backgrounds, had once attended the same school and shared the same environment and had been on an equivalent level of intelligence and education, his leaving at fourteen had tended to stop short his development at that point. He spoke with a broad Cockney accent, using ungrammatical everyday expressions that proclaimed him far less intelligent than I knew him to be. His talk was of dogs and horses and betting.

I was thinking how amazing the difference between us was when he said: "Ain't it funny, though. I could have been like you. I was nearly as good as you were at school, better than most. Look at me now. I'm a so-and-so tailor's presser. A lousy presser. Look at you. A muckin' writer. Look at so-and-so. A muckin' doctor. So-and-so. A muckin' solicitor. Look at muckin' me. Muckin' tailor's presser. And all because I left at fourteen and all of you were lucky and stayed on. I was just bloody unlucky, that's all, or I'd have been standing where you are."

He was right, of course. He had a chip on his shoulders and it seemed to me right that he should carry one. He had been unlucky. There, but for the grace of mischance went he, along with us. Or we with him, but for the grace of chance.

Looking at him, talking with him, I was more grateful than I had ever been in my life for the great gift of education. I didn't have the public-school accent. It was obvious from my speech that I was of East End stock. But my Cockney was not as broad as his. My speech had a more intelligent lift. My clothes were not so loud, my expressions and gestures less vulgar. Yet, at fourteen, we had been kin. We were out of the same mould.

We both knew we had taken different paths and could never really get together again. We were both a little sad. Both, of course, for the same reason: that his talent should not have had the chance it deserved.

He had been the breadwinner, he told me, when his father died. He had pressed from seven in the morning till nine at night to earn enough to feed and house his mother and his four younger brothers and sisters.

He had become a factory boy,

absorbing factory manners and behaviour, unconsciously following the speech he heard about him, consciously taking up the common pursuits of gambling and betting. He soon forgot all he had ever learned.

At fourteen the adolescent is merely on the threshold of knowledge. The doors are open. Then it is he can go forward into strange exciting new realms. Or turn back and retrace his road.

Bernie had retraced his road. The pity of it was that we both knew it.

We who stayed at Davenant until we were eighteen had much to be grateful for. A tradition of scholarship that set before us high standards of attainment we had to struggle to reach . . . but invariably reached, as had those before us and those who were to come after; outlets for our athletic pursuits — games, physical training; after school recreational activities such as debating, music, chess. The corporate spirit of the school was strong. Boys of my generation were proud that they went to Davenant.

But East End ways die hard. So, often in the weekends, the four of us — Shorty,

Hyman, Harry and I — would get together and start to play cards. Soon it became an event of great importance to us. We were all under its spell. Solo was the game — the East End's game. And is there a better card game?

Stakes grew higher as the games grew fiercer and Harry and I, who could less afford to lose than Hyman and Shorty, sometimes made fools of ourselves. Half a crown in those days could last a lad of our age for a month and often we lost it in a single night.

One day Harry lost 7s. 6d. This was the equivalent of a week's food for some families we knew. It was too much. But, in honour's name, he was bound to pay up. To Shorty and Hyman who were sharing his winnings he said: "Toss you double or nothing." It was a gambling challenge they could not very well refuse. Harry lost. He grinned. What was he up to? "Toss you double or nothing," he said again.

He lost about six consecutive tosses. The statisticians who claim that if you toss a penny a million times it will even itself out into about fifty per cent heads and fifty per cent tails would have had their faith a little shaken by the succession of wrong calls Harry made.

After a while the whole thing became absurd. When Harry owed them both 7s. 6d. to the 22nd power and was in debt to the tune of many thousands of pounds, everyone was laughing.

Eventually he won a toss and wiped out the bet. And in this way he taught us all how silly it was to play for money. We never gambled again.

Instead we went for walks. We talked learnedly about all sorts of abstruse subjects — philosophy, religion, politics, art, science — and considered ourselves just about the cleverest quartet the world had ever seen. Other boys could not, did not have our ideas. Other boys were not as we. We were unique. Four little gods strolling the Whitechapel Road and setting the universe to rights.

O time that has gone like sunspeckled shadows on morning walls. O where shall we find again the lost years, the lost companionship, the David and Jonathan walking under the street lamps through people-filled, thought-filled, nightridden roads? And the walking and the talking and the souls reaching out to know one another and understand. Now remembering heartsearingly we seek the once familiar language, the golden road into futuredom, the walk, the talk and the remembered face, the forgotten sounds. O time past and, by the tumbling years, amnesia-ed and analgesic-ed comradeship, let my memory hold you, reach you, relive you again. O golden, golden days.

Occasionally there joined us a non-Jewish boy called Allen. Tall, fair, fine-looking he was. Typically English. Stoutly Conservative. Turned up for cricket in immaculate cream flannels, knife-edged as to crease, wrinkle-free as to hang, and perfectly fitted. Club tie round waist. Cream linen shirt set off at neck by silk club scarf. For football in clean as a whistle togs. For athletics — at which he shone — in whiter than white vest.

Rank Tory. True blue. Blade straight. He was the one boy in the school who stood rigidly to attention during the playing of the National Anthem. We all stood, but only he stood ramrod stiff and sang every word.

We liked him. He was sincere, honest, true to his principles. We respected him. He would not gamble. Never cheated. Never swore. Did not even laugh when one of us, viewing a swelling bosom on a passing pretty maiden, said: "We didn't know what we missed when we were being breast-fed . . . what I'd give now to get my teeth into that lot!" Yet Allen was no prig. He was much too sincerely righteous to be hypocritical.

Some years later, long after I had lost touch with him, I was strolling through Hyde Park and came across a Communist rally. There, sprawled on the grass, with his bag and banner and belongings near him, and wearing the militant uniform proudly, was Allen. Allen the true blue. We looked at one another, said a polite few words of greeting and, both obviously embarrassed, departed.

I never saw him again. He was killed at Tobruk doing something daring and mad. Got a posthumous award. I've often wondered what happened to change Allen from a loyalist to a Communist and, presumably, back again to a patriot.

But gone, gone. The willow tree bent and the East End weeping. And no one remembering. No one remembering.

Being at school brought me into real contact for the first time with non-Jews — *Goyim*, as we called them. We mixed as though there were no barriers. Made close friends with boys of different religious beliefs. Worked and played together as if we were, which we were, all members of the human race. But, of course, Hitler had not yet arisen to stir up the muck heaps.

There were differences. Subtle differences. For instance, if one went into the home of a *Polak*, one would always be invited to join the family at meal times. In the short time one was there, one became a member of the family and was treated as such.

In the homes of the *Choots* there was less hospitality. A cup of tea could be regarded as a treat. And in the homes of Gentiles one could starve.

I had not then learned that Jews are regarded as stingy. I had heard jokes, of course; but since nearly all the good Jewish jokes I ever heard (and ever have heard) have been either Jewish in origin or by execution, I took this self-imposed sneer for a joke itself.

But when the years taught me that Jews were really regarded as miserly and stingy I did not understand. For of all the faults the English Gentiles possess, the greatest one is meanness. Yet, Goebbels-like, they have projected this failing on to others and, in accusing others of their own weakness, have rid themselves of their conscious fault.

The Salvation Army, hospital collectors, church fund raisers, Dr. Barnado volunteers, nuns and such-like came to Jewish doors in Broughton Buildings and were never turned away. It was the non-Jews who shut the doors in their faces.

Yet we in Broughton Buildings, who were much poorer than our Christian neighbours — for while their menfolk worked at wage-paying employment ours were itinerant street vendors or busy-time tailors and slack-time non-earners — lived better. Our money went on food and clothing. Theirs on gambling and drinking. Every Friday night we had chicken and they pointed at us and said venomously: "It's all right for those Jews — they can afford the best." Yet the chickens our domesticated, home-loving women (who knew how to cook) bought, cost less than the sides of bacon they sizzled away to nothing in their morning pans; far less than their daily gambles on the dogs; or their nightly drinking bouts.

As for cooking — the non-Jews had no idea. Light pastry was their limit. And O, so proud they, when they produced it; but of soups — nothing. Soup was something that came out of cans. Still does. Yet chicken soup — the most delectable of all the world's culinary mouthwateringnesses — comes from the water — water, yes water, yes water — in which the chicken is boiled. They pour it away. What do you know?

One of my friends was the cook at a fire station. One Christmas time they had amassed a lot of chickens and set about boiling them. Then they wanted to pour away the water. He fought to stop them. Succeeded. Served it up as soup. And the men licked their lips and said they had never tasted anything so heavenly.

During the war, when I was helping in the evacuation of children, I saw sights in provincial places that shocked me. London children, non-Jews all of them, were made to walk the streets till their meals were on the tables. They were looked down upon as slum brats though most of them came from better homes than those the war had pushed them into. They were cold and miserable and homesick.

In ugly Wolverton I wrote an article: *Open Your Hearts*. I begged the locals to think of the agony of suffering those little *slum brats* were going through. I was sent out of the town — dismissed the place.

My heart bled for the things I saw. But there was little sympathy. The rich kept their big houses uncontaminated, the working-classes opened them for the money received.

That was when I first began to lose my affection for the working-classes. Today I am an individualist, owing allegiance to none. I believe only in humanity and human beings. Yet I fear that humanity in the mass is vile. Only in separateness, in isolation, in men here and women there is there godliness and the big heart.

My East End was full of the big heart. Nowhere in the world was there a bigger. And now it is gone. Dust to dust and ashes to ashes.

The wind cannot speak as it whistles through town, but O the longing in its voice as it hurtles through the streets where once real people lived and my childhood passed away and the days went as if they had never been born.

13

Sex . . .

BUT whether you were Jew or Gentile, *Polak* or *Choot*, sex was common to all those who lived in Broughton Buildings. It was something you grew up with, as natural to you as eating and drinking. And it was never dirty. It was just one of those things you took for granted — like breathing.

When you sleep in the same room as that which mother and father use for their lovemaking; when, as so often happened in Broughton Buildings, your mother took in lovers for a living and loved them while the children supposedly slept; when you were brought up to learn of girls having children by their fathers and even knew a case where a mother had imbecile twins from her own backward louty son of seventeen, you certainly knew what sex was — whatever the word you used to describe it.

There was a little fair-haired blind boy who played in the yard. As children we used to tease him unmercifully. I remember that during the First World War we would terrify him by saying "Look out — the Germans are coming!" And the poor little boy would dash around, arms outflung, crying on his mother to come and rescue him.

But his mother was otherwise occupied. She was at that time one of the most notorious prostitutes in the East End — a ravenhaired majestic creature who had the policemen on the beat queueing up to try and seduce her. This was her little lost child. One of the benefits of syphilization.

He died before he was eight. By that time some of the glamour had worn off Black Bess and she was replaced by younger paramours.

She took a job as barmaid in the pub at the top of Goolden Street and there we would see her, big bosomed, heavy limbed, tall and still very desirable.

Big and strong for his age, was Jackie Pruse. His father was a boxer; his mother an ordinary housewife, busy enough looking after her six children.

One day we were watching the tots — boys and girls of four and five — pushing their bellies at one another as they played Mothers and Fathers, a very trite game even when played that way. We had seen it often. These kids were merely aping their elders. Nothing much happened till the children were at least ten years old. After that they went on playing the same games, but not in public.

One day, as I said, Jackie and I were watching the antics of these tots when Jackie said: "Ralph — have I got it bad!"

His emotional cornucopia was at bursting point. He could contain himself no longer.

"What, from watching those kids?"

"No. I've had it weeks. I must do something about it. I must. I'll go mad if I don't."

I suggested alternative alleviations.

"No. Not like that," he said fiercely.

"Then why not the real thing?" I asked. And he told me. Like me he was afraid of two things. One, getting the girl pregnant.

145

Two, catching a dose. The first could be avoided if one of the well-known women of the street could be bought, though they were curiously reluctant to accept customers who lived in the Buildings on the grounds, it seemed, that they did not wish to offend the wives they knew of the husbands who wanted to know them. But if pregnancy was avoided, venereal disease then became a major hazard.

So Jackie told me why he dare not try to ease his burdens, and I sympathized. I had very much the same problem all the time I lived in the Buildings and never resolved it.

We walked up Goolden Street together as dusk came. The pub at the top was not yet open. But in Goolden Street itself, in the long dark passage that led to the very innards of the pub, in the side domestic entrance as it were, lurked the leaning, lovely shape of Black Bess.

Loverly, to our virginal eyes anyway. Her thick hair falling about her nape and her low-cut frock bursting with its big balloons, her smallish waist, wide round hips and long length of well-shaped legs invited, almost demanded,

146

rapturous intimacy.

Jackie and I had long ago developed a theory: that the bigger the breasts of a pro, the slenderer her legs. Black Bess substantiated our theory.

Jackie stood there and ogled her as we went by. And suddenly she came forward out of the gloom of the dark narrow hallway and said: "What yer looking at?"

We mumbled a reply, I was for moving on. But Jackie stood as if paralysed. She grabbed his arm. Lucky for me, I thought even then, that he was bigger and better looking than I. In wild dreams many of us played at being Casanova, but when the chances presented themselves we shook at the knees and stumbled away as fast as we could.

"Come on, then," she insisted. "Come on in," she said.

I followed, uninvited, not daring to, yet unable to resist the possible outcome.

Half-way along the passageway she stopped, back against the wall, and Jackie stood facing her. I stopped a few feet away, barely able to breathe. She had forgotten me. She couldn't see me. But I could see her, dimly, because of the faint light that filtered down the hallway from the room far at the end.

"Well," she said to Jackie; "you're a big strong boy. *Like* me?"

Jackie mumbled something. And then he was lost. Lost in her big enveloping arms. Lost in the close physical contact. Lost in the shadows.

I couldn't leave. I was afraid to move, paralysed by fear and curiosity. I stood there petrified, watching, an unwilling yet willing Peeping Tom.

Jack was moaning. Black Bess bared her breasts, laughed; and fumbled for closer contact.

This was more than the tense, frustrated Jackie could bear. With a moan he collapsed, and I saw Black Bess recoil in anger at his failure.

She moved away from Jackie swearing coarsely, and he fell on the lino-covered floor, half crying, half sobbing, half hysterical.

Suddenly she was gone. Should I go to his rescue? But quickly she was back. Compassion had moved her. She wasn't all foul, seemingly. She produced a glass — whisky, I learned it was later — and made Jackie drink it down. Unaccustomed as he was to anything stronger than an occasional glass of sweet Palestinian wine, he choked and spluttered and coughed while Black Bess, restored to her good humour, laughed as she slapped his back.

Then she had hauled him to his feet and was pressing him against her. Now the tempo of things was unhurried. Bess knew even before Jackie did when their twin planets were in identical spheres.

He got up. She got up. "First time, eh?" she asked.

Jackie nodded and turned to go. I crept after him. We walked out together. "Come round again," Bess called after Jackie.

"Christ!" he was saying . . . "Christ!" over and over again. He was drunk with the excitement and thrill of having at last made it. Whoever said *"Post coitum omne animal Triste"* should have seen Jackie then.

But some ten days later he came running to me, his face shadowed with alarm.

"I've got it. I've got it. O Christ! Christ!"

And he had. Unmistakably. I told him to go to the Lock Hospital. It was confirmed. Syphilis. Two years of irrigations and mercury treatment. Two painful, frightful years. Two sordid, shameful years when he could barely look me, his best friend, in the eye; when he grew sullen, morose and introverted. A physical wound, that yielded to treatment for sure; but the mental one must have been incurable.

The benefits of syphilization. First time unlucky.

Then there was Gussy Green. Joined the army. Little Snotty, who never in all his life possessed a handkerchief, now had a uniform, and guardsman's to boot. He was a man at last.

He'd strut into the Buildings in his regalia and the kids would look at him in awestruck wonder.

Snotty went out with a bunch of his pals. Twelve of them all told. They found a girl in Hyde Park. A willing enough victim. Because of his youth and inexperience they let Gussy go first. They escaped, but Gussy got V.D.

In Broughton Buildings clap or pox were the daily sustenance of many.

And, as always, it was the mugs who got hurt most.

But I stayed clean and pure.

I was afraid.

14

. . . and More

DESPITE, or maybe because of the Black Bess incident, I resisted the stirrings of sex mightily.

I was afraid of consequences, that's all. Purity of mind was impossible in Broughton Buildings. Nor did days at school in the company of big, strong, unafraid youths help one's struggle to keep oneself unsullied.

Roger Bageot was always full of loose talk and looser tricks. Especially the penny-balancing act. He would balance coins in the most unlikely places. Lesson time was, for him, show time.

Those who could see him stifled their laughter and held their aching sides. Those who couldn't, guessing what was going on, used to turn quickly to catch the creased up faces and the watering eyes; but no teacher, as far as we guessed, ever suspected what was happening.

Or he would send flying out over the East End rooftops articles that looked like small balloons — but weren't. This was always good for a laugh.

By the time he was fifteen he'd had a score of women, mostly cheap prozzies — cheap, from the economical point of view, anyway, for he didn't have much money — and laughed at the suggestion that he could get a dose. His kind never got into trouble. It's true. It was the first timers who were always unlucky.

The best I'd done so far was Phyllis. Phyllis was a girl I'd met at my friend Jim Shelton's house when we worked there together doing our homework. Jim himself was sweet on her. But she didn't give him a second glance.

She came to see Jim's sister and managed to visit always when I was there.

Auburn haired, green-eyed, plump but well shaped, Phyllis was very pretty. I began to walk her home. After many such walkings I began to be invited inside the dark passageway of her house.

Naïve and inexperienced, I did not

know what to do beyond kissing, rather virginally, and sliding my hand down the front of her dress to feel her eager young breasts.

But when her parents began to invite me downstairs into the parlour and talk to me about my future and how long it would be before I made a living, I sent Phyllis a note and called it off.

I wasn't built for the role of a Casanova. Jim and Harry and many of my friends felt as I did. Women were all right to talk about and dream about and imagine how one could and would love them, but in reality it was best to save oneself for the one woman in your life. At least, this was our conscious get-out. I wasn't so sure about Hyman though. Women liked him. It would have been more difficult for him to convince himself that life held only the one woman for whom he must save himself.

From the W.C. window of our upstairs flat it was possible by standing on the seat, to gaze down over the area and the railings bounding it, on couples nestling in the dark of the playground.

Often I gazed, seeing nothing but

154

vague shapes and swaying shadows.

But one night I looked down and there was Milly Loss with a young man. Milly Loss was one of the most attractive young wenches in the Buildings. Beautifully made, with a handspan waist, upthrust breasts, fully formed, round, svelte hips and an eager, exciting face that housed a Joan Crawford wide-lipped hungry mouth, Milly turned many a head — mine included.

She and the young man were talking.

"No," she was saying, "I don't believe it. You're not a Jew."

The young man protested his Jewishness. But Milly wasn't having any.

Suddenly I heard her say: "Prove it . . . "

All alight with curiosity I craned forward.

"You mean . . . ?" stammered the young man.

But Milly wasn't going to say the wrong thing.

"Prove it!" she said.

He proved it.

Then the railings began to shake.

After this for many weeks the spot

became their rendezvous. Every night they stood there, kissed, fondled and made love.

I grew terribly frustrated watching it, yet could not tear myself away from the nightly vigil. And then one day it ceased. They did not make the railings shake any more.

I watched Milly. Looked for signs of pregnancy, within her. But her shapeliness remained unmarred.

My sister used to have friends in the house. Often the place was full of nineteen-twentyish young women showing far too much nineteen-twentyish leg for my comfort. Sometimes they even stayed the night.

I was home from school one morning, in bed in the upstairs flat which was empty, or so I thought, till I heard a movement in the bedroom next door.

Creeping softly to the door which was slightly open I saw Hilda washing herself at the wash-hand stand in the next room. Hilda was my favourite dream image. Dark, Spanish-looking, vivacious, curvaceous, exciteable, gay, her eager young mouth and lissom shape haunted me. And there she was. Practically naked.

I had stepped straight off my sofa bed and was in my pyjamas. The strain on my body loosed their cord and they fell around my legs.

The sudden sound brought Hilda round. She looked inquiringly towards the door but did not see me. I saw her, however, in all her agonizing appeal, an appeal so compelling, so irresistible that I could contain myself no longer.

Sobbing and demented I was spent before I had even kissed her or done anything more than lightly touch one of her nipples.

She fought free. I offered no resistance. Her eyes were aflame with anger. She was about four years older than I, but at that stage in our twin developments she was a woman and I was a child.

She was spluttering things like "How could you! You . . . you — of all people! What's come over you!"

Obviously surprised by my assault she had not yet had time to collect her wits.

I implored her not to tell my mother, to forgive me, to forget it, to keep quiet.

I couldn't tell her how the strivings of adolescence had rent me apart. I did not appeal to her to make an honest man of me. Contrite and shamed I humbly begged her forgiveness.

She stood before me, almost naked, a miniature goddess, a flaming dark beauty; and while I poured out my soul to her she went on with her toilet, twisting the flannel and curling it in and out of her ears.

She dressed while I watched and I was so bereft of all manliness that I looked upon it as though I had seen it all the days of my life — this beautifully attractive, seductive young woman reaching her stockings up to her pillared thigh, pushing her deep bosom into its artificial cups, swaggering into her corselet.

Then she was dressed.

She patted my head, as one pats a dog.

"It's all right," she said; "I won't tell anyone. But don't do anything like that again. Promise?"

I promised.

She patted my head again and she was gone.

I buried my face in the pillow and shook with shame, repression and vexation. She had treated me like a kid. I had meant nothing at all to her. Even the sight of my tortured body had not meant anything to her. She just looked upon me as a silly kid. Too silly to worry about, even.

And all the years after that when she came into the house we never by word or look referred to that incident again. But in my dreamings I acted like a man and made her happy with me.

15

Uncle Adolf . . .

UNCLE ADOLF was our favourite uncle. Even the later coming of a miserable repetition of this name could not obliterate our love for its first-known owner. Uncle he was because he had originated from the same Polish village as my mother. In the huge world of London that was enough to make him a blood brother.

Always as I remember him he was the best-dressed man in town. Immaculate from head to foot in well-cut suits, beautifully tailored overcoats, with a carnation in his buttonhole and a silver-mounted stick in his one hand, yellow gloves in the other. With his trilby set jauntily over one eye and his slim upright frame carrying all before it, Adolf looked a real man about town.

He was just that. Through the years I knew him he never seemed to age.

Young in heart, he told good stories, spoke of the shows, the films, the operas he'd seen; of the people he met.

Rake perhaps, but never a roué, Uncle Adolf was the brightest thing in our lives. He'd saunter in suddenly on a Sunday evening and light up the week that had passed and the week that was to come with his *bonhomie*, his wit and his good humour.

He was a Savile Row tailor who specialized in making military uniforms. Behind the shop where he worked he sat cross legged and hand-stitched the uniforms for royalty, the church, the services; for state occasions and ceremonials.

He was an excellent worker and therefore always in work. In those days that meant that he was a rich man. Certainly he could afford to send his three daughters away to school and have a housekeeper to look after him. He could afford to eat and drink well and to dress like a lord.

There had been tragedy in his life. His wife Thora had died in childbirth with the last child. He must have loved her a lot for he never married again though there were scores of women who would have grabbed him.

For he was handsome. His features were regular, and apart from a raised sort of small cyst just below his right eye — a mark of distinction it was on him — he did not have a blemish or a fault.

Opera was his grand passion. He had seen them all — Jan de Reszke, Caruso, Chaliapin, Galli Curci, Melba, Patty, del Monte. If his record collections seemed overweighted with the glorious voices of women singers it was not difficult to understand why. Possessor of a good singing voice himself, a rich rollicking baritone, he and brother Ben would engage in duets and a crowd would gather outside the railings below the windows and listen eagerly to the singing.

No Passover night was complete without Uncle Adolf. Even my grandfather held him in the greatest respect and would hold up the start of the celebrations till Adolf appeared.

He'd sweep in, as if to martial music, embrace us all, then sit down and join in the festivities. The ceremony of the Passover Seder Night ends in song. And Uncle would then let rip, leading the singing, recalling all the old buried tunes and dusting them off till they shone in splendour.

To this day when I am invited to a Sedar Night I can always end the celebrations on the right note by teaching those present the jolly, swinging, ringing tunes that Adolf taught us.

The traditional airs took on hidden depths of beauty under his chanting. And when the last note of the last song that marks the end of Seder Night for another year was reached, Ben and he and brother-in-law Alf (who had won competitions for singing) competed against one another to hold on to it. The note went on and on till we thought they would all burst; and Uncle Adolf always won. I am certain that my brother and my brother-in-law gave him the respect he deserved and let him win. And he would win joyfully, throwing his arms up and smiling all over his kindly face.

And then, with the wine already drunk at table and perhaps more to follow, he'd wax merry and recite us long passages from Shakespeare. These he declaimed majestically in that grand rich vibrant voice of his, rolling the fine syllables and the round phrases.

His favourite piece was a misquotation from *Lear*. This he would rise to do, his every gesture that of the monarch himself. Suiting his actions to the verse he would visibly swell before us as he cried: "And the thunder roared — de-re-re-re-rrrr, and the lightning flashed — se-se-se-se-ssss; and he cried 'Let the thunder be my friend, let the lightening be my comfort'!"

O it was terrific. It brought the house down. It brought applause from those gathered outside the windows to watch the *Polaks* celebrate their "Cider" Night.

And then we'd walk him home, my brothers and I, while he sang and declaimed his way along. Seeing a policeman he'd stop and point theatrically upwards and cry in his best Shakespearian, "Constable — what a lovely moon!"

O the gayness and the light-heartedness and the song and singing and the uplifted hearts. The wind shook the treeless streets. It was late March and the wind was shaking. March and there was a Mediterranean summer in our souls.

How easy it is to speak of suffering and poverty and sorrow. Our lives were not easy. But we didn't know they were hard. We didn't care that they were tough. And in that ignorance lay a balm that made poverty wonderful, even Saroyanishly beautiful. Certainly the Seder Nights of old were filled with magic and touched with the wonder that was Uncle Adolf.

All through our lives Uncle Adolf was there, part of the family. Breezing in at unexpected moments to dispel gloom and despair; descending on us out of the blue to ram music and laughter down our willing throats.

When the Second World War came, Adolf must have been in his sixties, still a fine figure of a man, still immaculately dressed, still full of good cheer and breathing optimism and faith and hope. He was living out at Dorking with one of his married daughters, and my wife and I, to get some respite from the continuous bombing, went down there for a week.

He was unchanged. He sat in the living room stitching military uniforms — the higher ranking ones, of course: admirals', generals', air marshalls' glad rags — plying a deft needle and singing to himself. He didn't look a day older. He was the immortal bard himself.

But at night Freda and I were awakened by the sound of crying. And there, in the next room, in his sleep, Adolf was calling upon his long dead wife. "Thora! Thora . . . O Thora!" he cried. We had never heard so much anguish in a human voice.

I leaped out of bed and ran next door; opened it; looked in. Uncle Adolf was asleep. His pillow was stained with tears. He was crying like a baby and threshing his arms and moaning and groaning.

We thought this was a nightmare. But the next night there it was again. And the next. And the next. And it went on. Uncle Adolf, the gay adventurer, the rake, the man about town, the never depressed, the light in heart, calling in misery upon his long dead love.

Freda and I couldn't bear it. It made us feel utterly utterly sad. O those cries.

They were heartrending, pathetic.

Yet, on the morrow, off he'd go for a walk, spruce, smiling, upright.

We couldn't bear it. How long, we asked his daughter, had he been like this? The answer shook us. Just one word. "Always."

What a sham was this then, this façade of laughter and song and good cheer. What sorrow in that smile. What a tale of love lost, and longing, and of a breaking heart. And the courage that put such a bold face on things, the resolve to live well with the world, to make it happier for his being there with you at any given time. O the heart worn inside the sleeve and the real aliveness that comes in tortured dreamings.

Always. Even in his singing. Always. Even in his Shakespeare. Always. At Seder Nights. At the opera. At *Macbeth*. At *Lear*. In his greetings to policemen. In his dealings with people. Always. The tortured lonely heart-breaking all these years.

He was sitting in a West End shop one day at a plate-glass window when an emissary from his cursed namesake, the other Adolf, burst before his eyes and he was shattered with glass and he died.

I have a conviction that if ever a man were willing to die that man was Adolf. He deserved to find his Thora waiting for him. He had clung grandly to life, making of it a bonny affair, a noble thing; but for the best part of his living, for all of fifty years, he had cried aloud in his sleep, calling upon the name of one he had loved and lost too soon.

And we thought he was the soul of good humour, the essence of wit. How wrong can you be?

Which of us has known his neighbour? Which of us has journeyed into his brother's heart? Which of us is not forever a lone stranger standing upon the borders of a land he can never rightfully enter? Which of us is not a ghost haunting a ghostly world?

And in the silent vastness of sleep we seek the lost world we hold but cannot touch, embrace the sought-after unfound vision, grope for the havens we never find on earth. In the emptiness of sleep there is anguish and sadness and tears that wet our pillows. But only in the unmeasured oceans of sleep is there hope.

O world invisible, intangible, incomprehensible. O my Uncle Adolf who sang so lustily and moaned in anguish all through the night.

I hear his laughter running through a million streets, I see him greeting a myriad policemen with his arms upraised to the yellow moon, I rejoice in his fine ringing voice bursting into song. And always always always always I hear his voice crying like an infant in the night.

Have you found your beloved Thora, Adolf?

Come, come, come to me Thora,
Come once again and be
Light of my eyes, light of my heart,
Angel of love to me.

Are you together again in some singing paradise of enchantment, together with a love that defies time, or do you sleep silently in an apartheid of forgetfulness where even love like yours is buried deep and nothing, nothing has life?

Rest easily, O Adolf. I will remember you.

16

. . . and Others

WE called Adolf "uncle", but in fact we boasted few relatives. Most of our uncles and aunts had been acquired. They were the soberer, more intelligent, more personable portion of the lost army that used our home as its barrack room, its canteen and all too often its dormitory, too. Searching eagerly for roots we had picked up the livelier pieces of flotsam and jetsam that moved down the tide of existence to an unknown destination, harboured them in our own backyard and ennobled them by giving them a relationship.

There was old Axelrodt, a tenuous gremlin of a man, bent, beak-nosed, rheumy-eyed and shuffling. Like an overgrown leprechaun with swollen belly and bright blue eyes ever peering, ever darting, Axelrodt became an uncle because he could talk sensibly. And my mother could never resist the good talker. It mattered not that he spoke Rumanian, one of the few languages my mother did not speak or write. Their converse was in Yiddish, that universal link between kindred souls.

Yiddish is a fine, expressive tongue. There are things you can say in Yiddish that you cannot say in any other language. Even in polite company you can swear in Yiddish. Its oaths and swear words are expressive, full of imagery, explosive with scorn or contempt or scathing. And in Yiddish they are an accepted part of normal conversation.

America has borrowed freely from Yiddish. Such words as "gelt", "mazumah", "shemozzle", "pinochle", "stumer", "shmaltzy", "shamus", "Kibbitzer", "spiel", and the latter day appendage of "nick", which derives from Yiddish word-endings like "paskoodnik" (no-gooder) and has been tagged on to Americanisms like "beat", are Yiddish in origin.

In Yiddish you can cry while you speak. The language is full of heart-rending phrases. You can rant. You can fill your speech with similes in a way that even Gerald Kersh might envy.

And to hear Axelrodt and my mother speaking of many things in their beautiful Yiddish that was a song, a dirge, a lament, a wail and at the same time a cascading torrent of laughter, was to know the living beauty of language.

Axelrodt had few words of English. He was a testy man who took to himself testy phrases. His favourite was "Seddan!" "Seddan" he would shout at me when I interrupted. "Seddan" when anyone riled him. "Sit down" it meant. Sit down we did.

Axelrodt came often to our rooms. He sat reading his Yiddish or Rumanian papers in a corner, waiting till my mother had come in from the barrow so that he could talk. He ate his meals with us. He stayed late.

He came and went as an accepted member of the family. Nobody had much to say to him. He was a widower. Somewhere he had a son. He had no other living kith and kin. If he worked or had a trade we never knew. How he lived we never knew. For years and years he was part of our household, as were so many more. And then he did not come any longer. We heard that he had died alone in a back room somewhere off the Mile End Road.

Then there was Mr. Lewis. A pock-marked, red-faced, red-nosed rough diamond of a man whose looks belied him. He had the sweetest nature of any man I have ever known. He never said an unkind word, never raised his voice in anger.

He too was a lonely man. My mother had developed this knack of sheltering the lonely. She found them by the handful in the byways of the East End and gave them what they craved for most of all in life — a family they could call their own. Another mouth to feed? What did it matter? No one queried her doings. Mother knew best.

Lewis was a night watchman. Which meant that his days were spent with us and that he did not leave us till night fell. We liked old Lewis. He loved us.

He too came and went; and one day did not come any more. We sorrowed at the news of his passing.

Axelrodt and Lewis were nonentities.

But they were human beings. Life had been unkind to them. Torn from their homelands, they remained forever strangers in a strange land. Neither of them ever mastered the simplest parts of English. Neither of them made friends. Axelrodt was too bad-tempered. Lewis was too shy. Both were human misfits.

How many of us are strangers and alone. Shut tight into the shells of our own making we are part of a world that washes over and about us and whose fury finally rolls us up into a deserted part of the human beach. And there we lie, prisoned by the world and our own spiritlessness, ourselves the prisoners, alone and a part of the incommunicable, inimical earth.

O waste of living in the busy days, the dark nights, the changing seasons. O lost among the bright stars. What are they these passengers through the convolutions of living but a falling leaf, a forgotten face? Lost and unremembered ones who never lived, who never joined themselves to the core of being, who were dead when they were born and dead when they were growing up and dead when they died, but then dead for ever. Fixed in no time they have no memorial. Their living, their being, their no-doing are of no account. O forgotten faces that never were.

There were many like these two who seemed to have inherited nothing but loneliness and sadness. They came into the house, rescued by the big heart of my mother. And some of them stayed and some went their way.

The unmarried Mrs. Simons stayed. She was a thin, pale, ginger-haired wisp of a woman who looked as if she would fall to the first puff of wind.

Mrs. Simons was ill. She was always ill. She clutched her stomach and moaned. All the time she moaned. She went in and out of hospital, was cut up, about, around and over. Her thin, wasted concentration-camp-like body was scored with a Hampton Court maze of scars and stitches.

Yet she was indomitable. She moaned but she never lost hope. In her frail body there beat just about the toughest heart in all the world. She always came back for more. If only some of our boxing heavyweights had had her courage.

We liked her because, in her broken English, she was fluently descriptive. She gave us running commentaries on our neighbours that flamed with colour. And she loved ceremonies and celebrations. She would come panting back from a wedding to tell us "De brite vore a tray so long dat de paidboys falled over it — it was boonival, boonival. Und de broom he say to his vorkfolks 'Haf de days off'. Den he gif his regadds to his stuff and off dey vent in a car viff a chopper. O it vas vunnerful . . . !"

My sister Betty used to curl up in knots and listen entranced to Mrs. Simons's excitement as it poured out in a steady flow of crippled English.

Between bouts at hospital, Mrs. Simons worked as a seamstress. My mother would say that she had "golden fingers". She managed to keep her Sammy well-fed and to live reasonably well.

And she did not die . . . not for many, many years. Not till she had seen her Sammy married and have a child — another Ginger Sammy — and become the master of his own barber shop; not till she had herself married for the first time and found at long last some reward in breathing. Her later years were healthy ones. Her illnesses fell away from her. She put on weight. In her late forties she grew almost beautiful.

I like to think that here was one soul my mother plucked from the torrent who finally learned to keep her own head above water.

Our real relatives were few. But there were the Butvenks of Bath who were related in some vague way to cousins of my father and to Adolf. Uncle Joe had done well. He owned a couple of shops in Bath and was quite the richest man we knew.

Whenever he came to town it was an occasion. He had a couple of very charming daughters and a fine son. And we were fond of his wife, Anna. Our place was too small to put them all up; but in any case Uncle Joe could afford to stay at a hotel.

On the occasion of my eldest sister's wedding, however, it was decided that Lionel, the son, should share a bed with me. The excitement of the forthcoming wedding had us all in its grip. Sleep was the last thing any of us wanted.

My brothers and Lionel and I played cards until well into the morning and then reluctantly we made our way to bed.

Lionel was in great form. He kept telling me funny stories that had me guffawing and cackling till dawn.

Suddenly he grew serious and began to talk about marriage. He was then about nineteen, a well set up, darkly handsome young man with a lovely head of black wavy hair and bright black eyes like twin lumps of flaming coal.

Marriage, he told me, was not for him. He would not marry. Not ever. I pressed him for the reason. And then he turned his back on me and farted. I was so astonished I nearly fell out of bed.

"That's why", he said. "How can you marry and suddenly fart in bed? You couldn't do it. You couldn't do it, that's all."

I protested that he could marry and do it. Tell his wife. Warn her. Prepare her for the terrible shock.

But he was adamant. He was deeply

conscious of his inability to hold his wind and, beneath his levity, I could detect a certain sadness. He had convinced himself that he had a weakness that barred his right to future happiness.

I laughed at him. I reasoned with him. I tried to show him that he was making a mountain out of a molehill. "An explosion out of a puff," I remembered telling him.

But he would not be comforted. Under his extroverted madcap self he was inordinately shy and self-conscious to the point of being neurotic. I remember getting mad with him. "You've got a bee in your bonnet about wind in your arse," I told him. He laughed. I see him now. The black head of hair thrown back, those dark eyes; his teeth minstrel-show white in the grey light.

The subject changed. He began to tell me more jokes. I fell asleep for a while and when I awoke he was still laughing over the last funny tale he'd told.

He went away and never came back. During the war he was drowned in the North Sea when his ship was torpedoed. It was many years after the long night of storytelling. In that time he could have married and reared children, gay little urchins with laughing eyes like their father.

But he never married. The wind and the wind stood between him. And looking back now I don't find it funny. I can't raise a smile. It's not a theme for tragedians or a Shakespeare or even one of those angry young men who have so little to be angry about. As I am angry now when I think of Lionel the lonely . . . lonely because he farted in bed.

Lonely now in the cold depths of the North Sea. Lonely and alone. All alone.

17

Practical Science

GROPING his way myopically through the last places of every form in the school, a bane to his teachers and a delight to his colleagues, was Jim Shelton. I am sure he could have persuaded even Lionel to lose his inhibitions for he himself was not only completely uninhibited, but one of the most persuasive talkers I have known. He could certainly sell us, his schoolmates, anything — even an idea.

He was the son of an Irish woman and a cockney policeman and had inherited the brashness of both: the quick mind of his father and the idleness of his mother, the ugliness of his father and the charm of his mother, the keen sense of his father and the short sight of his mother.

He was also torn between being forced to be a devout Catholic and wanting nothing more than to be an irreligious

Protestant as his father was.

He was clever. We all knew he was clever. But his attitude to school work was that it was a bore. He just wanted to grow up quickly and become a policeman like his father; and he knew that he would never be one because his eyes were bad. So, from an early age, he lost interest in his future and in most things. He was one of the most disinterested people I ever knew.

He had a shrewd scientific brain. At chemistry and physics he was outstandingly the best in the class. Yet when the examinations came he would never answer more than a couple of questions. Half-way through the exam you could see Jim doodling on his paper or picking his nose, that faraway Irish look in his eyes.

He had a sister, Eileen, three years older than he, who was a real beauty. She had inherited her mother's good looks without her mother's myopia, and she was a yellow-haired, white-skinned temptress who had all the adolescents in the school mentally seducing her every time they saw her and often when she wasn't even around.

The combination of Jim's scientific turn of mind and his sister's undoubted attractions produced a situation that had our form queueing up for many weeks to be friendly with him. Especially as Jim sold us her beauty so convincingly that even those who had never seen her were in love with her.

Not only was Eileen beautiful — she had already, at the age of eighteen, won three face and figure competitions — but she was surrounded by lovely friends, girls of her own age from the dramatic and dancing school she attended. Phyllis, with whom I had conducted a fearful flirtation, was the youngest of this party of pulchritude. Some of the girls often stayed the night with Eileen, for the Shelton's lived in a big house off the Whitechapel Road, a house with rooms to spare that had once been the station house and was now given over entirely to the four members of the Shelton family.

Which meant that we liked to be invited to Jim's house; but the girls, most of them our seniors by a few years, and far more sophisticated than we were, would never even look at us let alone talk to us. Phyllis had been the sole exception. The others didn't seem to know we existed.

It was Jim who first thought of spying on them. When he told us what he had in mind, we gaped at the devilish boldness of the scheme but never thought he would have either the courage, the apparatus, or the opportunity to put the mad idea into practice.

One day, however, he invited six of us to his house. We sat in his bedroom before his dressing-table mirror and were able to see right into the big bedroom that Eileen and her friends were sharing. They were, as I remember, dressing for a dance and their motions, their twists and turnings sent us crazy with excitement.

Roger Bageot was so overcome that he couldn't sit still.

How had Jim arranged it? With a series of mirrors, starting with one fixed high in the girl's room and another against the fanlight over the door and a couple across the corridor and so on, each catching the reflections of the whole room from the large dressing-table in Eileen's room and reflecting the vision farther afield.

So that we could sit in Jim's room and watch the girls and enjoy stifled delight. Television by mirrors before TV was even thought of.

A week later and Jim had hastily summoned us round again. The girls were off to another function. And this time Jim had an even greater surprise. He had mirrored up the bathroom.

Other episodes concerning Jim Shelton stand out clearly. There was the day we made chlorine in the lab. We made it in tall glass cylinders which we covered with a greaseproof circle of glass. We were strictly enjoined not to sniff. Chlorine was the gas used in the First World War. It was dangerous to smell. Thus we were warned.

Next thing we knew Jim was coughing and spluttering and rapidly going blue in the face and almost semi-conscious. Naturally he had taken a good deep sniff. Naturally. Had he not been told not to? A prohibition was all that Jim needed. It was a green light to him. We had to rush him across the road to London Hospital, five of us lugging him like a sack.

They told us he was nearly a goner,

too. It was three weeks before he was able to come back to school.

Then there was the occasion of the Annual Speech Day. The Mayor of Stepney was present. The Chairman of the Education Committee. Local councillors. The local M.P. The local editor of the local news sheet. Professors. Dons. Dignitaries. And one especial guest of honour, the dowager marchioness of something or other, an old crone with a bevy of older cronies supporting her presence.

Big Hall overlooked a small quadrangle. Across the way, about the length of a cricket pitch away, were the labs.

Suddenly the putrid stink of rotten eggs began to fill the tightly packed hall. The hellish smell swelled and packed the place. People grew hot, uncomfortable, embarrassed. Men loosened their collars. Women fanned themselves. But the stench was all pervading. One woman in the audience retched. Everyone looked blankly at everyone else.

Then I remembered. We had been making H_2S — hydrogen sulphide I think it is called, or something like that — in the lab. the day before. We had made huge retorts of the stuff. And someone was there filtering it our way. The wind was in the right direction and consternation had been caused.

Catching Hyman's eye I found we had both hit the same solution. We edged our way out of our seats and sprinted across the playground and up the stairs. The door of the lab. was locked. We beat upon it with our fists. A shamefaced and frightened-looking Jim Shelton opened up. He had not only pointed the retorts in the direction of the Big Hall open windows but, after opening the taps, had been fanning the gas on its way.

Quickly we closed the windows, closed the taps, put the retorts back and hustled Jim out of the place and back into the Hall. The stink was still almost unbearable. But, gallantly, proceedings went on. By common silent assent a blind eye was being turned to what a blind nose could not have avoided. And, within a little while, the smell died away.

Next day the Head had the whole school assembled. Some nasty little boy had thrown stink bombs. What nasty little boy had done this nasty little thing? What nasty little boy had ruined Speech Day and made the school ridiculous? If the nasty little boy did not come forward the whole school would lose the half-day holiday that was an annual outcome of the annual Speech Day celebrations.

But no nasty little boy had thrown stink bombs. The nasty little boy had done something far worse. Something that meant his breaking into the locked laboratory and tampering and tinkering with dangerous gases. We could not let Jim tell. Hyman and I stood either side of him to hold him back. There was no need. He made no attempt to tell.

The school lost its half-day holiday and the incident was forgotten. We all decided that the laugh was worth while. Even now I feel sure it was.

It was Jim too who was responsible for a succession of teachers having to jump from their chairs in agony. And how the class laughed as teachers peered closely at the chair seat, seeking the upturned drawing pin that we, as "big boys", would never have used. Such tricks were beneath us.

Three teachers came in for lessons on three different occasions, sat on their seats and jumped. They looked. They peered. They groped. And in each case none of them went back to his seat for the next hour.

But the fourth, rotund Herr Bandt, the German master, was made of different stuff. Three times he sat on the chair and three times he screamed like a demented fishwife.

"Brass Band" was already a butt. Which German teachers are not? He lost his temper too easily. And the more he lost his temper and the more he raved, the more did his classes torment him. Nearly every lesson with "Brass Band" was chaos and havoc. Choss and haverack. This lesson went apart in its first mad moment. As Herr Bandt leaped from his stool there was a wild high outburst of laughter. Then the hysterics began from him. And the shouting and yelling and chaffing from all parts of the class.

The class was screaming itself hoarse

by the time Bandt had leaped for the third time. He threw the chair over and practically tore it apart. And he found the wire cleverly running up one leg and under the seat cover. The wire that came through a hole in the small carpet on which the chair stood and ran under the desks to the inside of Jim Shelton's desk where a powerful accumulator was feeding it live current.

So clever was the camouflage that none of the other teachers had seen the wire. And neither would Brassy have done had he not pulled the chair apart. Then, as the German master marched up the line of desks to follow the trail, came to Jim's desk, opened the lid and saw what was concealed there, a hush fell over the class.

The next moment it was drowned by the squeals of Jim. Bandt had seized the bare wires and placed them against Jim's face. Jim yelled. Put up his hands to protect himself. The wires were put on his hands, on his ears, on his head. He screamed and twisted in torment.

Suddenly Bandt tore the wires from their sockets and threw them out of the window. All at once he sobered up. For Jim was burnt. The livid injuries were plain to see.

Herr Bandt suddenly looked terrified. He began to excuse himself, saying that Jim had only himself to blame, that he should not have got up to such dangerous tricks, that he, Jim, could not blame him, Herr Bandt, for what had happened.

Jim had never meant anyone to take the force of this current on unguarded skin. The powerful accumulator and all the other electrical gear Jim had crammed into his desk was meant to produce shock through a covering of clothing. On bare skin its effects were serious.

In the silence broken only by Jim's whimperings, Herr Bandt took hold of Jim's hands and said: "Come — let us go tell the Head what has happened."

And Jim looked up and said: "No. I won't say anything if you won't. It serves me right, sir."

That's how it ended. Jim carried some nasty burn marks around for a few weeks; but even before they went he was already plaguing "Brass Band" as much as he had been wont to do.

Jim went on to become an optician. He opened a small shop in Mile End soon after he had qualified, which he did easily enough, and eventually branched out in other districts. He now has a chain of optician shops all round London. And whenever Eileen breezes into town they see one another.

I read about their meetings in the newspapers every so often and I think of the harum scarum Jim and his beautiful sister. But far more of the beautiful sister. As she was, of course. She is handsome now, but not the ravishing beauty of twenty years ago, or the luscious, unforgettable lovely that Bageot attempted to rape.

I wonder how that eminent architect Roger Bageot reacts when he hears of her these days? I know how I do. I think immediately of the past and I wonder if any boy ever had a more crowded, more diverse, more entertaining, harder and more sorrowful upbringing than I? But not so much of the sorrowful and the painful. Only now do I see how more favoured and fortunate some are. And yet, not so much more fortunate, for my days were full to the brim with living, and in those days I was never aware that life was tough, or that I was going short of so much that was given to so many.

Life was full to the brim. And even the nude perfection of Eileen's slender young body did not make the day of my seeing her any more memorable than a succession of memorable days.

All those days were memorable. All my friends were fair.

And then they came, the days of sighs and laughter, the formless fancies in a vale of tears.

Now purpose was apparent in things and life seen as a bitter struggle to survive. Now it was plain the weakest went to the wall and life was to the strong if it were to be lived to the lees.

Now came living and it was a confused affair. Sometimes smiles ran high and sometimes tears stung the eyes.

And always always it was a puzzle, a question, a perplexing unsolvable riddle. Why? Why were we here? What was the point?

In those days, verging towards manhood and alone, life was incomprehensible.

In those days it was hell. But, occasionally, heaven too.

18

Gigolo

THE most colourful, the most exciting and the most fantastic character of my life in those days — perhaps in all my days — was Jerry Short.

Poor old Jerry was so tall and so bad at games that the kids used to call after him: "Who knocked the wicket down? Longtom! Who knocked the wicket down? Longtom!" From which you will gather that the only time Jerry had attempted to play serious cricket he had been a laughable failure. He swiped out so crudely with his bat that he broke the tops off all three stumps. At football he was clumsy, awkward, all big feet. Useless at games, was Jerry. The butt of his fellows.

His early life had been really tough. We reckoned that we lived in the lap of luxury compared with Jerry.

His father was a drunkard and womanizer. He beat Jerry unmercifully when he was drunk and that was most of the time. One night, coming home drunk, he attempted to seduce his own daughter, Jerry's elder sister, a black-haired, sun-tanned lovely, and Jerry went to Ruth's rescue.

There had been a fight. And what a fight. Father and son had gone for one another with everything in the house. Mr. Short broke a chair over his son's head. Jerry kicked his father in the groin and his father went into hospital and after that was never any good for women again.

They lived right at the top of a Broughton Buildings tenement. And when Jerry left his father moaning on the floor he himself was so badly injured, his head cut and bleeding, one arm broken and two ribs fractured, that he could only crawl down the many flights of stairs like a wounded animal.

He told his sister to fetch aid for his father and crawled away to lick his own hurts.

When he got down to the bottom he could not stand, so he crawled into the cellar among all the rubbish and smells and garbage and rotting food . . . into the dark, damp cellar which had only three walls and one side open for the once-a-year dustmen to venture into . . . crawled in among the rats and collapsed.

My Booba first heard him moaning and sent for my mother who sent for my brothers who brought him out and sent for a doctor. He was rushed to hospital. He lay there with rheumatic fever for six months. When he came out his sister had become a prostitute, his mother had left his father, his father was pimping on a coloured whore and Jerry refused to go home.

So he became our lodger. Just another soul to house and feed for free. But only for a while.

He was fifteen then and shortly afterwards began to earn money. He went to work doing anything that would bring in an honest living — crane-driving, market-portering, paper-selling, errand-running — and took a little room somewhere and managed for himself.

He was so independent. He was about

the most independent person I have ever met.

And because he had been taunted for his lack of grace he took up ballroom dancing. He was determined to prove that he could excel at something. And he was very determined.

He had inherited his father's fierce, explosive temper. I was standing with him one day in the Whitechapel Library Reading Room, he a tall bony lad of seventeen and I about thirteen at the time, and he was studying the Employments Vacant column in the *Daily Telegraph* when a huge navvy, all of six feet six in his socks and the best part of fourteen stone of solid muscle on his body, pushed Jerry roughly aside with the remark that Jerry had had the muckin' paper too muckin' long and wasn't it about muckin' time he muckin'-well mucked off.

Jerry remonstrated. The navvy put his big flat hand on Jerry's pigeon chest and just pushed Jerry backwards, hard. Jerry picked himself off the floor, walked over to the navvy and as the navvy, seeing his aggressive attitude, squared up, Jerry hit him with the hardest right-hand punch to the jaw I ever saw. The navvy went down as if poleaxed. His head struck the tessellated floor with a crack. He lay prone, unmoving.

Jerry seized my arm and we made our way out. Ten minutes later we heard the ambulance. Next day's papers told how a navvy had been set upon and beaten up while minding his own business in a library reading room. He had sustained a fractured skull. But he would live.

I was terribly worried. Saw police at every corner. Grew anxious at every knock. Could not stop from thinking the man would die — and then what?

But Jerry did not give the matter a second thought. He would not have cared if the navvy had died. When occasion demanded he could be cruel; and afterwards ruthless and unforgiving.

Some months after this episode I was walking with Jerry when he suddenly stopped, told me to wait a moment, walked over to a car that had pulled up at the lights, hoisted the driver through the window by his tie and collar, hit the man a terrific left-handed uppercut, dropped him down, and left him slumped over his seat as though dead.

He returned to me metaphorically dusting himself down, for he said: "That bastard fired me for nothing last week." And we walked away. There were no repercussions.

It was this ruthless inability to forgive or forget that made Jerry take up ballroom dancing with such determination to succeed. Soon he was winning small prizes all over London. And suddenly he was news. He came third in the Star Ballroom championships.

Now he emerged. All the pent-up repressions were at last given free rein. He womanized like mad. He dressed well. He moved out of the East End to a West End flat. He kept older women company and was paid for his services.

We thought he was a bad 'un. Like father, like son, we told ourselves. Yet Jerry never forgot us. At least once a week he would come back and spend hours with us. He gave me all his books — and that bare statement of fact really covers most of the beginning of my literary education. For Jerry was a self-educated person who had really taken to education. He loved being knowledgeable. He enjoyed learning for learning's sake.

The books he gave me were so many and so varied that I had no room for them. They finally found a home inside the ottoman on which I then slept, a sofa-like contrivance that opened up and revealed a coffin-like space that, when the books were placed in it, was filled to the rims.

There were some two hundred and more books. For the next five years I did not lack for reading. It was good reading, too. Tolstoy, Chekov, Dostoievsky, Proust, Meredith, Thackeray, Sterne, Fielding, Smollett, Boswell, Dickens, down to Rider Haggard and Henty. IIis taste was eclectic. It shaped my own.

It proved again that if Jerry set out to do anything, he did it.

He took up judo, demonstrated a neck hold on my brother-in-law, Alf, and had to be torn away when Alf, his eyes goggling and his face turning blue, was almost on the point of collapse and already sagging.

He took up fencing and was dismissed

his club when, losing his temper, he began to use the rapier as a stick and flayed his poor opponent into a state of terror and semi-unconsciousness.

Although never very strong in health — rheumatic fever and early malnutrition had left him internally weak — he rippled in hard muscle. He had grown still taller, but his shoulders were broad, his waist narrow; he had slender hips and had developed an easy elegance, a casual air, possibly through dancing, that turned feminine eyes adoringly his way.

Dark, lean visaged, with dark brown smouldering eyes that shone and a strong chin that lent him masculinity, Jerry was a walking Rudolf Valentino at a time when his similarity to Hollywood's darling stood him in good stead.

His dancing improved. Ben took lessons from him. Mark and I watched. His feline grace, almost panther-like in its ease of movement, his slender carriage, those broad shoulders pirouetting — these and his decidedly handsome face made him a striking figure.

How far removed he had grown

from the "Who-knocked-the-wicket-down-Longtom" gangling youth whose awkwardness had made him a butt. He had shown the world he could be graceful. He was the most graceful man I ever saw; more graceful than Hobbs at the wicket or Bunny Austin on the tennis court. He walked in beauty like the night. Every step he took was a line of poetry with rhythm, lilt and lyricism.

Ah, but he was lithe and lissom. And sinewy and willowy and strong. Ah, but he was good to look upon.

He became famous when he won the Star Championship and went on to win the All-England Amateur title. Now he had arrived. Now his face stared out of a thousand advertisements: Jerry Short uses this, recommends that, tells you this is good, that you should buy that. He was photographed with motor-cars, dogs, women. He mixed in high society. His handsome face and elegant figure appeared in the glossy high-priced magazines.

He went to Savile Row for his clothes and never did clothes make a better man that they made Jerry Short. He looked like a million dollars.

The leading men's wear trade paper chose him as "The best dressed man in Britain". The leading national daily chose him as "The handsomest man in Britain".

He was offered acting parts, but refused them, preferring to concentrate on his dancing. He had made up his mind to become the best dancer in the world. He was also propositioned. To such unholy suggestions he had one reply — his vicious right fist.

Having won all the amateur honours he turned professional. And that's where he made his fatal mistake. That, coupled with the change in his personal luck, was the beginning of the end. For the red-haired partner who had shared his triumphs became pregnant and Jerry married her. He did not love her, but he thought he ought to marry her. Ruthless and cruel though he could be, he was yet in many ways a person of high principles. In his position very few men would have married the girl. Jerry never thought he should do otherwise. The child, a red-haired boy, was called

Ben, after my brother. Zaida did not approve. And said so forcibly.

To find another partner was no easy matter. So much of a perfectionist had Jerry become that no woman made the grade as his dancing partner, even if they made it as his sleeping partner.

His peculiar sense of ethics told him that he had done right by marrying the mother of his child but that he would do no wrong by continuing to live as he had lived. This he had made clear to his wife. She, glad enough to be made an honest woman, acceded. Whatever his failings, Jerry would never have lived a life of deceit. If he lived wrongly he at least insisted on living truthfully. His dishonour was rooted in honour. Unfaithfulness kept him faithfully false.

Why did he turn professional?

He told us one night as we sat into the early hours of the morning in the front upstairs room which looked like a parlour and which, as soon as Jerry was gone, would be hastily converted into our bedroom.

He told us that he could never make any real money as an amateur. He could win lots of gifts which he had to pawn to turn into money. He could be paid for figuring in advertisements, but this money was irregular, unreliable and would not go on for ever. He had no trade. Dancing was his profession; therefore it was logical to earn money at it.

But brilliant though he had been as an amateur, as a professional Jerry was one of perhaps half a dozen exceptional dancers most of whom had had more professional experience.

In those days it was the amateurs who held the limelight. The professional dancers were unknown to the general public. They went on the stage, or gave exhibitions in night clubs, or taught their skill in schools of dancing.

Jerry's dancing was too straight to make stage entertainment. He had one week at the Coliseum, danced up and down the stage with immaculate technique, his partner in his arms and following his steps, went off to mild applause only, and his engagement was not renewed. People did not go to the theatre or the music hall to see ballroom dancing. Adagio dancing, acrobatic dancing, ballet dancing . . . but not ballroom dancing.

He became host at La Splendoure, one of London's leading night clubs and restaurants.

Now when he came to see us at Broughton Buildings he led two magnificent borzoi hounds out of an elegant chauffeur-driven Rolls-Royce, and in his beautifully tailored Savile Row suit he looked like a duke or an earl. The Broughton Buildings crowd gaped at him open-mouthed.

How could he do it, we wanted to know, on his salary, however good it might have been, at La Splendoure?

He didn't tell us. But we knew. He was being kept by a succession of women. My brother Ben went to La Splendoure as Jerry's guest; came back to report that a stream of aged crows, dripping diamonds and jewels, almost came to blows to dance with him; that they passed him money after every dance; that they passed him keys too.

Jerry was spending every night of the week with a different woman, most of them old enough to be his mother. Those who weren't, were old enough to be his grandmother.

One night at La Splendoure someone called him a gigolo. Jerry brought over that lethal right uppercut and sent his jeerer crashing through upturned tables to lie still on the floor. It turned out that his victim was a lord with immense power in the city during the day and even greater influence in the night clubs when day was done.

Jerry's brief hour of glory was over. No other reputable night club would employ him. He finally got a job as Mine Host at a second-rate hotel. He lasted a month. Again someone taunted him. Again Jerry somersaulted his taunter over the dining tables. This time he also emptied a bottle of wine over the fellow. And forgot to open the bottle.

He spent three months in jail. Ben and Mark visited him regularly. So did his wife who loved him a lot.

When he came out life was tough. He was reduced to selling everything he had. The women he had slept with refused to be made love to by a jailbird. They wanted upper-class fornication.

Jerry finally took a post as Master of Ceremonies on a cruise ship. His job was to keep the unaccompanied women accompanied. The boat did four ten-week trips each year, steaming into the sun so that, even in an English winter, the vessel was crowded with fun seekers.

He danced till three every morning and slept with one woman or another till noon the following day. When the restaurant began to fill up for lunch, Jerry had to be back on duty to chat and talk and fill the lives of the lonely.

He was a bad sailor. He was sick most of the time. He couldn't bear being cooped up in tiny cabins with crones sweating all over him. The unceasing mechanical routine of never-ending dancing was getting him down. As were other things.

After three trips he was in bad shape. We saw him when he came round to Broughton Buildings during one of his spells ashore. He was thin and peaked. He looked terribly tired. But he was making money.

He had signed on for a year and he meant to keep his word. So he went back for the final hot summer cruise.

Jerry was no drinking man. He had not many virtues but this one he had. Yet the captain repeatedly accused Jerry of being drunk. He was unsteady on his feet at this time, his co-ordination had gone, his muscles wouldn't respond to his mental stimuli and he was a sick man.

Finally he could stand the captain's tauntings no longer. At the breaking-point cry of "You drunken sot!" — last of a succession of suchlike sneers — he chinned the captain.

He was put in irons after being severely manhandled by some of the crew who had never liked his smart ways. They put him ashore at Marseilles. He hitch-hiked his way back to Southampton.

He finally made London, collapsing in the street where the lorry driver who had taken pity on him set him down.

He was taken to London Hospital.

His heart gave out and he died two days after being admitted. Ben and Mark and I were round the bedside when he died. He looked at us, smiled, murmured weakly "Who knocked the wicket down? . . . Long . . . tom . . . !"

Then he turned his face to the wall and died. Swiftly, gracefully, like the dancer he was, his soul left his body and went waltzing away.

He was only twenty-eight when he died. His crowded hour of glorious life was an age of struggle against impossible odds. From the beginning Jerry was destined to suffer. If he took the easy way out who could blame him?

His name was writ on water. Today nobody remembers him. Nobody thinks about him. Yet he was the most graceful man who ever lived, beautiful in his elegance, lyrical in his movements.

He had an uncontrollable temper. He was amoral. Yet I and my brothers remember him for his determination, for his courage, for his fight against the raw deal life handed him and for the way he never forgot us. Even when he was rubbing shoulders with high society, his heart and his home were in Broughton Buildings.

Principles he had. He stood firm by his word. He was loyal after his fashion. We liked him.

Given the right sort of upbringing and family affection, Jerry might have been a different man, perhaps a better man. But would he have been such a colourful character?

Jerry dancing. The slender, lissom grace of him. Jerry winning awards to a storm of applause. Jerry, the scorned, the jeered at, earning admiration. Ah gone now. Gone gone. Young, immaculate, handsome Jerry, gone. But always young, always handsome, always immaculate. In that way he has cheated time.

I hear a waltz and it is Jerry's waltz and I see him moving over the floor with all the grace of a ballerina, all the lilting rhythm of a line from Swinburne, all the heart-searching loveliness of imperishable melody. He was the dance. His body and the dance were primevally one, together as one since the beginning of time.

Born to dance, he was. To be the acme of lyrical loveliness in movement. To prove that man can be manly and beautiful and full of form and grace and richness. To be blessed with the poetry of the foot.

Ah, but he was good to look upon as he danced. There was beauty, there was.

19

Smiler Pocker

JERRY SHORT, although he had time for only few people, always, even when he was famous and busy, found time for the blind man at the top of the street.

Blind Simka had been blind since the day he was born, he said, and he was called Blind Pete.

And he was some sort of gay character, short and broad and chubby with laughing lips. He had a heavy pock-marked face, somewhat villainous-looking I must admit, but forever creased in smiles. "Smiler Pocker" the kids called him.

He sat at the top of Goolden Street where it meets Aldgate High Street and sold boxes of matches from a tin tray. Because he was blind he was an obvious target for my mother's great compassion; and because he was blind he never really needed it, at least not as much as old man Lewis and the withered Axelrodt and the pain-wracked Mrs. Simon and the army of misfits who were always being fitted into our house.

For people took pity on him and bought freely from his tin tray, often forgetting to take the box of matches they had bought. Blind Simka was just about the most contented man I ever met. He had everything, he said, a man needs and wants. Seeing? What was seeing?

He was married to a neat little woman who kept a neat little home for him in the three rooms they rented near the London Docks. The place was spick, span and comfortable. He was better off than we were!

He had a habit of humming to himself as he sat at his pitch in all weathers staring at the passing world out of his sightless eyes. Even when it rained or snowed, even if it blew hard or cold cut razor-edged, he sat by his tin tray singing snatches of old songs. Of his boyhood in Lithuania he sang; old Jewish folksongs; German Lieder; and "When Irish Eyes are Smiling". Especially "When Irish Eyes are Smiling". Maybe it was the bit about eyes that took his fancy. For his own translucent eyes were always smiling too.

His customers, and he had lots of them, called him "Blind Pete". They were sorry for him — my mother was not alone in her big-heartedness — and they bought often. And as most days he left his pitch in the evenings, leaning on his wife's arm, with just about as many boxes of matches as he had started with and a pocket that jingled merrily, blindness for Simka was not such a terrible thing, especially as he did not realize that he was different.

At least, up to a point. For he knew that he did not understand people when they talked about colours. And this made him angry and sometimes a little hurt. He tried desperately all his life to know what colours meant and honestly believed that if only folks could explain themselves the whole thing would be clear to him.

Reds, blues, yellows, greens — what were they? And why couldn't someone tell him?

As he loved the weather, all weathers — I have seen him sitting all covered in snow like a peddling snowman — I never missed him on my way to and from school. He was always there. And even when I tried to pass him, because I was late, or because I did not feel like talking to him, he would know me and call me and I'd have to stop.

"Boychick" he called me, using the familiar Yiddish diminutive to show affection. "Boychick ... come here. How's mum? And Ed? and Mark, Polly, Ben, Betty, Lily? And your Zaida and Booba?" Had he missed anyone? Not he. He counted us off on his stubby fingers.

And then, inevitably, "Tell me about colours today, boychick. What's blue?" he would say, staring at me with his pale shining eyes. "What's blue?" And not only blue. "What's yellow, red, green, violet, white and black?" he also wanted to know. He wanted to know so much.

From the age of five upwards I talked to Blind Simka about colours. From that early age I knew how impossible it is for the blind to appreciate just what colour is. The idea grew up within me. I never stopped thinking about it.

When I was getting to be a young man and had grown more fluent and confident, I made strenuous attempts to teach him colours. Even then I did not realize it was impossible.

"What's blue?" he asked me one day. "What's blue, boychick?"

I gave him my tie to hold. He fingered it in his stubby hands, using his hands and fingers in that flat-handed way the blind have.

"So that's blue . . . that's blue," he said; "all kinda soft and silky. Well, that ain't hard. Why didn't someone tell me before. Now, what's yellow?"

Just like that. "What's yellow?"

"Like the sun," I said.

"Sure. I know. Warm and nice and comfortable on your bones. And red, boychick? And red?"

He was so eager. This smiling man's face was creased in excitement. His eyes were alight.

"Red?" I said; "like a tomato."

"I know. Soft yet hard. Smooth. Slippery. And now tell me white, and black and . . . ?"

I said nothing. How could I? What was there to say without hurting him?

"Come on, boychick," he said. "I'm getting it. Don't let me down now!"

"You don't get it at all," I said. "You haven't got the faintest idea what it's all about. You don't even begin to understand. Colours aren't touching. They're seeing."

And then, I shall never forget it, he looked at me with his sightless eyeballs and grabbed my hand and said plaintively: "What's seeing?"

That's all he wanted to know. Only that. Such a simple thing. "What's seeing?" Go on, tell him. Tell tell tell tell tell him. Seeing is . . . It is . . . If you look . . . Look? What's look?

Where did you start and how did you go on and what was the finish?

I began to shout. I told him he never understood a thing. I told him he was deluding himself. I called him stupid. I am ashamed of that still. Stupid, I called him.

And he held my hand tight and said: "Don't get upset, boychick. I'm not upset. I'm not worried. So we're different?

So what? How different? I eat like you. I breathe like you. Look, I can hold you with fingers and hands like you've got. I walk. I sing. Where's the difference? I'm happy. I love my wife. It's a good life. Got a good wife and a nice home. Make a living. Know nice people, like your mother. God bless her and may she live long and have *nachas* (good fortune) from you all. Don't get upset with me, boychick. Maybe because I never went to school I never learned about seeing. But if only people wouldn't keep talking about it all the time."

I felt humiliated. Like a little child who has lost a favourite toy. I had another try.

"You know about time, don't you, Mister Simka? Like twenty to three and five past seven and all that?"

He nodded. "Sure I do."

"Well, sometimes you ask people the time, don't you?"

"Yes. Surely."

"And what do they do?"

"They tell me the time."

"Yes, but how do they tell you the time?"

"By the clock," he said.

"That's it!" Now I was triumphant. "That's it. They *look* at their watches and tell you the time. *Look; see* — get it?"

"And so can I . . . "

He pushed back his coat and brought forth a watch. I watched him run his fingers over it and then he looked at me with a wonderful grin of achievement all over his pock-marked face and he said quietly: "It's twenty to six."

Desperately I took his face between my hands and turned his head in the direction of the big clock above Gardiner's Corner.

"Over there," I told him, "there's a clock. It's up on a high tower and it's about a hundred yards away from here. And right here, from where I am standing, I can tell you the time by that clock. That's what people do when you ask them the time. They look over there, all that way, and tell you the time. They don't touch anything. They just turn their heads and look and they can see what the time is even when it's far away. Now do you understand?"

He shook his head. We were both close to tears at that moment. "No. I don't. How can they touch it all that way away. They can't. They don't. Then how can you possibly tell the time if you have nothing to touch? But I know they do it. I know, I know. That's what worries me. That's why I know they can do things I can't. So that's why I asked you in the first place, *what's blue?*

"That's all I want to know. What's blue? Go on, just tell me what blue is and I'll be a happy man."

And there it was. I used to go home and think. Think of all the good things he missed. Little things. Not the big things like the dawn coming up like thunder or dusk falling over the grey tenements. But a chair in the park, just an ordinary everyday chair. My Booba's tired, worn, weary face lit by love for her grandchildren. My Zaida's wonderful grey-black beard. Little things. A couple of toddlers walking hand in hand. The way the showers washed the streets. Shop lights gleaming in the rain. Paper blowing about the streets. Candles on Friday evening and the white cloth and the brown patterned bread and the red wine. Reflection in a glass, in puddles. Dancing sunbeams. Even shadows.

Little things. The sharp point of a pencil. A newspaper's headline. The flickering cinema screen. Kids playing football with a paper ball; cricket against the lamp posts. The colour of The Lane on Sundays, the blaring, jazzy Lane that was the gateway to Samarkand. People's faces when they were glad, sad, worried, angry, ashamed. People's faces. O the wonder and the seeing and the looking in them. Windows. Door knockers. Paving stones. The cracks between them. Wisps of fragile grass. A light being switched on. Lamplit windows in the mauveness of a rain-swept East End twilight. Twilight itself, indescribably soft and brown as the linnet's wing.

He saw nothing. He wasn't living. Not really. I used to think for hours, for days, for weeks, for months, for years. And finally I got it out of my system by writing about it. And nobody cared.

But I cared. I cared about Blind Pete. I used to cross over the other side of the street to avoid him because he made me feel so sad. And little by little I stopped seeing him.

And this tale has an ending. It has a number of endings, but it has one fine last one.

After the blitz and the end of the war I was wandering through my old haunts, crying a little inside me for the way Broughton Buildings was no more, thinking of all those people I'd known who were killed and wondering what happened to Blind Simka called Pete, when I saw him.

There he was, sitting at his old pitch outside a bombed building on the corner, but sitting in a wheelchair.

And I just had to go over and talk to him. He knew me at once. Knew me by my step. Grasped my hands, pulled me down, kissed me. He looked so frail. He was getting on for seventy then, and I noticed new scars on his face cutting right across the pock marks. He was thin and weak.

He told me he had been in the blast line of a buzz bomb that fell on Aldgate towards the end of the war. The raids he had escaped. His wife had led him to shelter. But the buzz bomb caught him. Blew him into unconsciousness. And when he woke in hospital it was minus both legs. His face had been badly cut. He had severe concussion. Three ribs were fractured. His right arm had been broken and he showed me how it had healed at an angle so that it hung out of true.

And then he looked up at me and smiled and his sightless eyes danced and he said: "I'm lucky to be alive."

Lucky to be alive. Blind, crippled, disfigured, maimed. Lucky to be alive.

I ask you . . .

20

Like a Fish

MR. HEWSON always said he, too, was lucky to be alive. And he looked it. Mr. Hewson stopped, as so many did, at my mother's stall, intrigued and fascinated, no doubt, by the earnest discussion group in being.

He stayed to talk; found that his knowledge of German enabled him to understand the trend of the conversation whenever it turned aside from the broken English to Yiddish; and ended up by following the rest of the crowd into our flat to continue the argument.

After that Mr. Hewson — we never discovered his first name — was a frequent visitor. And when he chanced to tell my mother that he suffered from some stomach ailment, ate little and had to be very careful what he ate, mother invited him to take his daily lunch with us — not not-to-feed him, but to fuss him.

Thus, for years and years, Mr. Hewson came in at twelve-thirty and sat around till two-ish. He was the first non-Jewish regular member of the Finn family. And nobody gave his non-Jewishness a thought. Nor did he ever, by word or inference, suggest that he was doing something unusual by lunching with a Jewish family.

Mother liked him because he was an intelligent man. He was a solicitor in the City. A comfortable man, financially speaking; a most uncomfortable man, physically speaking. As he sat he screwed up his legs, winding them tight round one another, and shook them to and fro, to and fro, never stopping for a second.

I used to watch his long interwined tickling legs with the same fascination as any youngster would watch the inside of a clock in motion.

Why did he do it? Because he was always in pain. His stomach never gave him any rest.

All night long he would lie, he told us, on his back, staring at the ceiling. He had lived so long with pain that he was able to bear it. His will-power, he said, was like iron. He could deliberately deprive himself of the little pleasantries and comforts he most wanted.

He not only talked but looked like an ascetic. He ate hardly enough to satisfy a butterfly . . . a leaf of salad, a glass of cold milk; yet this apology for a meal would seem to give him strength, to join in argument and conversation.

He it was who contributed to the greatest moment of voltefacedness, turn-aboutness or inversion, call it what you will, I had until then witnessed.

Zaida used to gather around him the wise men of the congregation. All day long they would talk deep, learned, obscure philosophical talk and argue abstrusedly on unrecognizable subjects.

Among these wise old men was one, Rab Yossel, who had not said a word of note for twenty years. He was said to be very wise indeed and considering carefully the words he was to use that would, when uttered, startle first his congregation and then rock the whole planetary system to its very foundations.

One day the old men were talking about Life . . . with a capital L, of course. Talking earnestly and devotedly and absorbingly and wholeheartedly and passionately about Life. Talking in a broken mixture of Yiddish and English.

We stood by listening, enjoying the solemn attempts to sound inspired if not inspiring. Mr. Hewson smiled tolerantly at their seriousness.

Suddenly Rab Yossel cleared his throat. Everyone looked up. Was the oracle about to speak? At last . . . ?

It was!

Rab Yossel was speaking. In a thin childish treble he was talking, with great gravity and syllabic solemnity. And he said: "Life is like a fish."

They stared at him hard. They shook their heads. "*Life is like a fish.*" So what is this tremendously of significance, uh? If, for sure, Life is like a fish, then is maybe the meaning is p'r'aps as Life must be very deep . . . Or p'r'aps Life is like a kind of some sort of an underwater kind of living? . . . Or maybe it is that with too much breathing it is a way to make one stupid? . . . Or how would it be p'r'aps if Life went round in little circlets? Ain't it? P'r'aps it might be, no?

You could almost hear them thinking in their peculiar and involved convolutions of speech as you watched their sad, serious, solemn faces pondering this infinite truth that twenty years of deep thought had finally crystalized into words in Rab Yossel's brain.

"*Life is like a fish.*" Like a fish. Not like an animal or a plant or even a human being. But like a fish. Like a fish. The moment of truth. Of wisdom, of understanding, of knowledge.

It needed thought. It required concentrated study. It was a revelation, a semi-divine utterance. Even so had the great Rabbis of old spoken. In veiled words and riddles. Thus had the Great Truths come that shook the world.

The silence was profound. You could have heard a pulse-beat.

And then, with a smile on his thin lips, Mr. Hewson said quite politely: "You know, Mr. Yossel, I don't believe Life *is* like a fish."

They looked at Mr. Hewson and began to deliberate the wisdom of this point of view, so diametrically opposite to the Great Thought itself.

This needed careful consideration, too.

And suddenly Rab Yossel cleared his throat again. Everyone was tense and expectant. What wonderful thoughts was the learned one now about to utter? With what cryptic remark would he devastate the non-believer?

And Rab Yossel hunched his thin shoulders and spread wide his thin arms and said in his pipsqueak voice: "Well, maybe Life is not like a fish."

Then there was silence.

When I think of Mr. Hewson I think of this. The picture takes shape in my mind. My Zaida and his henchmen. The thinkers. The talkers. The actors who had for so long told themselves they were setting the world to rights that they truly believed they talked about matters of prime moment and weighty importance. And the way Mr. Hewson threw a spanner in their works.

For years and years he came to us at lunchtime and complained about his stomach and did not eat and everyone said he had cancer. He was so thin and yellow. And then we heard that he'd been taken ill. There was nothing wrong with his stomach. But years of malnutrition and neurotic insomnia had broken his health. He died in three weeks of galloping consumption.

There were many other non-Jews we knew; but we did not like them half as much. The police, for instance. Every Sunday they would go down the Lane and its environs in pairs. And from each stall holder they collected half a crown. So afraid were these migrant Jews of the police, that nobody ever shopped them or refused to pay. If you refused, you lost your pitch. No matter if you had been standing in the same place for the last twenty years (as all good market men claimed they had), the police would remove you from your pitch unless you greased their palm. Bribery was rife. Yet to those who had known the more ruthless police forces of Continental countries, the London police were wonderful. Provided you paid them, they kept their word. There was no attempt at extortion.

My brothers and I once computed, after following the police (at a safe distance) down the Petticoat Lane, into Goolden Street, through Wentworth Street, Old Castle Street and other adjoining streets, that their haul at the end of each Sunday totalled well over fifty pounds!

Did they have a share out at the station? Under the eagle eyes of the inspector, perhaps?

There were also, of course, the visiting gas and electricity men who came periodically to empty the penny-in-the-slot meters — it was some years after moving into Broughton Buildings that we had electricity installed. And the coalman, milkman, postman and dustman were non-Jewish. Each one of them, in turn, knew that there was always a cup of tea and a biscuit waiting for him and his mate at our house. Many a time I have seen the dustmen, covered still in the remnants of their trade and reeking to high heaven, sitting in our chairs — our couches that were our beds! — and sucking away at their cuppas.

Did they ever think my mother was a mug? Or were all the Yids mugs? For while the non-Jewish residents never even gave them a thank-you and the

233

Choots were but mildly polite, the *Polaks* treated them with kindness and over-consideration. In praise of these borough council workers and junior civil servants, I must say that I cannot remember any of them ever taking advantage of our weakness.

In fact, the problem of anti-Semitism never arose. There were non-Jews in London, of course; and, one assumed, in the rest of Britain and the world. The 'bus and tram drivers, for instance. People one passed in the streets. But one never gave a thought to any conscious difference. There was no difference. People were people. Until Hitler began to tell them they were not.

One of those who had experienced anti-Semitism was Kirschenbaum — "Old Cherry Bush" as we called him. He was a tall, saturnine individual with a drooping black moustache in a long, gloomy, sallow face. He looked like an anarchist. And he was.

Kirschenbaum was a chemist. Qualified, too. He had a shop opposite Dorset Street, off Brick Lane. It had Russian calligraphy painted across its windows and was known as the Russian Pharmacy.

Kirschenbaum had been a doctor under the Czar. One of the few Jews who had been allowed to qualify. He must have been a brilliant medico; he was certainly an exceptionally fine chemist.

He often told us of the hurts and torments he had had to endure in Russia: of the patients he was compelled to treat who refused to pay him because he was Jewish and whom he could not take to law. Of the taxes he was made to bear that beggared him; of the time when he was thrown into prison for refusing a drug prescription to an officer in the Czar's regiment.

He had smuggled out of Russia at the age of thirty. Found himself penniless in London. Worked as a porter in the market and went to evening school at night to qualify. But he had realized soon enough that a British medical degree was beyond him and had switched to pharmacy. Saving hard he had managed to open the Russian Pharmacy. Such wonderful advice did he give to those who came to him seeking remedies, such fine prescriptions did he dispense, that he was idolized in the district. People never bothered to call a doctor. They went to "Old Cherry Bush", related the first-or second-hand symptoms and were given the magical prescription that nearly always cured the ailment.

At times Kirschenbaum must have steered pretty close to the law by carrying out the duties of a qualified practitioner of medicine; but this was none of his doing. He had a soft heart and could never refuse the tearful pleas of women who demanded that he visit their sick husbands or children.

He hated all forms of law and order. Argued fiercely with my mother and then, in the same breath, proposed that they live together in the free love he believed in. My mother was still a very handsome woman and "Old Cherry Bush", although no picture painting, was a tall, upstanding man . . . and he could have kept both my mother and her brood in relative comfort.

Obviously in love with mother, and often declaiming to her passionately in Russian, Kirschenbaum was finally compelled, against his better judgement perhaps, to offer my mother marriage. It seemed the only way. When she refused, he went off to marry someone else and quickly raised a family. But he never stopped visiting us and we liked him. When we had toothache he would even pull our teeth, he often pulled our ears, and occasionally greased our palms with copper.

Many many years later, when Mosley tried to march through the East End, "Old Cherry Bush", then nearing sixty, was one of those who organized to stop him. He himself stood before the marching blackshirts and engaged them in combat. He was severely cut across the head by a heavy stone but went on flinging missiles and defiance back at the marchers, his head pouring blood.

During the Second World War this hater of authority tried time and again to get into the army and finished up as an air-raid warden. He was honoured during the blitz for rescuing four people from a bombed building.

The honour came too late. The building fell about his ears and he died. Still hating authority, I've no doubt.

21

Dossen Street

KIRSCHENBAUM'S shop was quite close to the notorious Duval Street. It is in the news again. A murder has been committed there. The papers are full of it as I write.

I remember Duval Street. It was called Dorset Street in those days. The foreigners found this difficult. They called it Dossen Street. And what a good name it was. The street was all doss houses.

Dossen Street alias Dorset Street alias Duval Street still smells as it did apparently. Rows by any other name . . . (and whether you pronounce that "rose" you're still right).

It was a street of whores. There is, I always feel (though lexicographers, philologists and magistrates' courts do not uphold my contention) a subtle difference between an whore and a prostitute. At least we used to think so. Prozzies were younger, more attractive. Whores were debauched old bags. Dossen Street was full of debauched old bags. It teemed with nasty characters — desperate, wicked, lecherous, razor-slashing hoodlums. No Jews lived there. Only a few bold *Choots* had the temerity even to walk through it.

There were pubs every few yards. Bawdy houses every few feet. It was peopled by roaring drunken fighting-mad killers. Jack the Ripper (Jack Dripper, my Booba used to say) had once killed one of its whores on one of its dingy doorsteps. Every night near murders were done. Police refused to patrol it except in threes. Ambulances, fire engines and police wagons rushed towards it every night.

Even my Zaida, afraid of nothing though he was, refused to walk down Dossen Street. The hoodlums would have torn his beard from him and lynched any bearded man who ventured two yards into it. As youngsters we used to dare one another to walk down Dorset Street. Only once did I try. Kids, ragged and filthy, ran at me from all sides. Women swore at me from windows. I went about five paces into it and was out again in a flash.

King of the street, the Al Capone of Dorset Street, was a tall gipsy-looking man, dark visaged and evil, who was known as Blackie Ferret. He had the most frightening face I ever saw, a nearly black pock-marked skin, criss-crossed by livid razor scars, one of which ran from his beetle forehead right down his cheek, across both lips and wound itself round the bottom half of his chin on the other side.

He was a leader of a race gang known to the police and all of us as the Aldgate Mob. They were razor slashers who frequented the racecourses and made their money by protecting bookmakers — or else, or by waylaying winning punters.

Mighty slick with a razor was Blackie. One of his favourite pastimes was to walk the East End with a tray of flags, as though he were selling for charity. He'd walk up to the unsuspecting passers-by and hiss: "Flag, lady?" "Flag, mister?" You dare not turn away. He'd stick his ugly mug right into your face and repeat his request with emphasis. If you were adamant you would get slashed for your pains or your handbag or wallet filched before your very eyes. Most people paid up. Those who didn't went yelling for the police, clutching their slashed faces and crying for lost possessions.

The police must have had enough on Blackie and his mob to put them away indefinitely. Yet Blackie continued to walk the streets and terrorize the inhabitants.

He had three women in Broughton Buildings, three prozzies he kept in three different flats. In turn he would visit one, the next day the other and so on. One day he left all three with their cheeks slashed and running blood. They met in the centre playground and screamed hysterically, the blood running in three streamlets to make a red pool at their feet. Police came. Ambulances came. Blackie went on walking the streets.

We were burgled one time. Mother came home from the barrow to find that our upstairs flat had been cleared of clothes, candlesticks, ornaments. It was a common occurrence. One good heave at a Broughton Buildings door and it just gave. An intruder could walk in and help himself as he pleased.

The next day Blackie was at the stall with a bundle.

"Mrs. Alec," he said; "one of my boys nicked this little lot. When he told me where from, I did 'im. 'Ere y'are, Mrs. Alec. Them wot hinterferes wiv yer'll get what's comin' to 'em."

Even the great Blackie respected my mother. I do believe *she* could have walked down Dorset Street and no one would have moved an inch to impede her progress. She never tried, but I am sure she was the one person in the whole of the country who could have done it.

One day even Blackie went too far. They still talk about the Battle of Wentworth Street . . .

Running across the bottom of Goolden Street and into Petticoat Lane is Wentworth Street. Here Blackie had a fish stall. Most days he was not there. His henchmen looked after it. Just on this day he was.

A woman did not like the fish he was

offering her. So he slapped it round her face. No one could accuse Blackie of selling stinking fish. She did not know Blackie. She called a policeman. The copper did not know Blackie. He was new to the beat.

He got obstreperous. Blackie slashed his face. We were on the way home from school and we saw it all.

The young policeman blew his whistle. Over went the fish stalls, a whole line of them, about twenty all told, and within minutes the entire side of that part of Wentworth Street was a barricade behind which the fishers crouched, waiting for the cops to arrive.

Down Goolden Street roared the wagons. Out came a posse of cops. Blackie yelled. And the cops were showered with fish and lumps of ice. They drew back against the facing wall. Above that ran a continuation of the Broughton Buildings tenements. And from overhead women showered water and worse, the contents of babies' potties and bed pans, over the hapless cops.

Reinforcements were sent for. Soon one side of Wentworth Street was ranged by a couple of hundred police. The other side by a barricade of upturned stalls.

When the police tried to rush, a hail of ice met them. Ice can be a dangerous weapon. Lots of intrepid cops were soon smothered in blood.

Then it got bad. One cop hauled a woman down from an upstairs window for breaking a glass vase over a colleague's head. As he jostled her around the front of the blue line, Blackie threw a fish knife and pinned him, right through the forearm, to the far wall.

That was the signal for fish knives and razors and broken glass to be thrown and some of these fishers, many of whom were in the Aldgate Mob, were pretty dab hands at throwing.

From where we were, huddled in a group at the end of Goolden Street, too terrified to run, too fascinated to tear ourselves away, we watched the grim battle proceed. When the fishers ran out of ammunition they began breaking up the pavement behind them and sending over large lumps of jagged concrete and asphalt.

The police were powerless. Showered

on from above, assaulted from the front, they stood their ground, dodging the missiles. Soon a number of them were stretched out cold on the roadway.

Then the firemen arrived. It was the beginning of the end. They got their hoses going and, as the jets mounted, one by one the upturned stalls were swept back against the wall. Behind them, tight against stone and shopfronts, the fishers crouched. But they could not answer the terrifying power of the water. The stalls were swept away. As the men started to run they were bowled over.

The police went in with their truncheons. They were merciless. Every fisher who showed fight was clubbed down. Skulls were cracked like bad eggs.

Blackie, bedraggled and yelling defiance, was set on by a dozen stalwart cops. They beat him to his knees and went on beating him to a pulp. He lay on the floor, bleeding and still, and then they began to kick him.

The ambulance men came and stretchered him away. The street was cleaned up. Blackie was in hospital for six months. In jail for only three months after that.

He was out again, one arm still in a sling, a wide bandage round his head, looking more venomous than ever, and sticking his tray of paper flags under people's noses with a "Six-pence — or I'll slash yer face!"

The night he came out there was a riot in Dorset Street. The gutters flowed with blood. Police came in and carted away a group of unconscious men who had taken over Blackie's territory. He was back. Flags flew over top and bottom of the street. The undisputed king of Dossen Street was in residence again.

Villain though he was, Blackie gave a lot of money to charity, endowed a bed at the Brick Lane Infirmary and ended up in it himself that night during the blitz when he insisted on rescuing a cat from the third floor of a badly bombed tenement house.

And because he was such a villain, Blackie lived. Only the good die young.

So people grew up and in the growing seemed to lose part of themselves. In the throes of adulthood one never lives again the wild fervent impulsive days of childhood when each hour is a fantasy and each day an adventure.

In the young the uncontrolled sailing is towards uncharted mains, to flower-strewn islands where one may eat of honey dew and drink the milk of Paradise. In the older, the sailing becomes a constrained voyaging between known points. To go farther is to seek that unknown bourne from which no traveller returns.

And if there is any reaching out, it is towards fulfilment and death.

So people grew up in their fast approach towards extinction. And days that had been were somehow tinged with the roseate hue of sunset. And even if, if the truth be told, yesterday was a vale of tears, distance has turned the tears to laughter.

O there is fun in remembering, and sadness too, and sorrow. But in looking forward there is only finality.

So people grew up and were less wise,

less imaginative, less happy and more old than they had been. And that was yesterday, so it was good. And now it is today, and only tomorrow is good.

Yet if the logical sequence of mathematical time is followed to its cold, pure solution, there is far more in yesterday than there can be in tomorrow. So people grew up, I among them. And in looking backward found something to hold on to, and in looking forward found only the unsolved riddle of time and a faceless, nameless clutching at the heart.

For what future is there in the future . . . ?

22

Brown Bird Singing

WHEN he was a boy my brother Ben had the voice of a bull frog sitting on a lily pad and calling to its mate. He never made the school choir. He never even made the class choir. Nor the synagogue choir. Even at home we told him to shut up.

Maybe this rankled Ben. Yet I don't know. He was never a lad who grew rankled. He didn't take offence. A nice, easy-going sort of nature he had and most people liked him. I liked him except when he used his superior strength to browbeat me. But that wasn't oftener than is normal with most boys.

He was a terrific reader in his early days. He devoured the printed word. And he read so fast. One day, curious to know if he really read every line, I turned over about thirty pages of a book he was reading. Ben came back, sat down, and went on reading where I had left off! We chuckled about it for years afterwards.

He already wore pebble lenses and his eyes got so bad that for a long time he had to stop reading altogether. Not that Ben minded this, for he was able to skip school and find time, as I have told, to put colouring matter in Bully's lemonade bottle.

He was keen on games. He swam well. He represented the school once and my sister Betty, standing near me, was praying aloud: "Please God, let him win, let my brother Ben win." But he came in last just the same. He swam strongly but slowly.

He took up judo, which he practised with Jerry Short, and could fall through the air with the greatest of ease. He tried cycling, cycled to Brighton and back on his first real day out on a cycle, came home, threw himself on a bed, slept the clock round and did not cycle again.

He learned dancing, also at the skilled feet of Jerry Short, and was always, from that time on, a better dancer than most. The trouble was that Ben grew very tall and, then fully grown, nearly split his partners with the enormous strides he took. Shades of the twist: in those days the good dancer strode the floor in seven-league boots. Ben took mighty strides and refused to dance on a crowded floor.

He was good at his school work, good at home, had a rare sense of humour and, despite his bulk, disliked violence in any shape or size. He was a gentle giant.

But he could not sing. And he wanted to.

Then, suddenly we began to hear him sing. Not that he sang well. But he sang. He suddenly began to burst into song at all hours of the day. It was unbearable.

He had just left school and was working in a radio and record shop. He brought records home and played them. His taste was good. Even from the start his taste was good. The voices of Caruso, McCormack, Chaliapin, Tito Rufflo and other great ones filled the air.

And Ben would sing with them, spoiling the wonder of their voices with his own croakings. His voice had just broken and he was pretty rough on the ear. We ragged him. But he went on singing.

He began to get better, too. He began to get so that we could listen to him without flinching.

Then he took lessons. At the boys' club we attended there were classes. Ben went regularly. They thought he showed promise when we were still thinking he showed clearly that his voice had broken from rough to grating.

And his improvement became noticeable. Now and again he was worth listening to . . . for a bar or two. And slowly, slowly, his voice matured. The roughness left him. The new voice took on a rich tonal quality. He began to sing tenor and in the higher reaches his voice was distinctly pleasant, nasal like Richard Crooks (one of his heroes), but pleasant.

Now he was on the road, travelling, doing the job he was to do for the rest of his days (and still does so successfully), and he was away from home for a week at a time. But each time he returned we noticed the difference in his voice.

At the annual Seder nights it had always been a contest between Uncle Adolf and my brother-in-law, Alf, as to who could hold longest the last note of the last song on the last night. Soon Ben could outsing them both, though his inner politeness always made him defer to Adolf at the right moment.

Now he could sing so that we wanted to listen to him. Now he joined operatic societies and took lessons from better qualified teachers and studied the technique of the great and learned about phrasing and breathing.

When I think of the easy success that comes the way of our beat singers — the hundreds and thousands of pounds a week they earn for opening their mouths and making pleasant noises . . . sometimes — and of the way brother Ben sweated to learn singing, how to pitch the voice, where to breathe, inflexion, cadence, harmonics, *sotto voce*, *crescendo*, control, flexibility and a score of other technical necessities, I am amazed that success can come so easily in one sphere of non-singing and have to be so hardly won in the sphere of real singing.

Not that this bothered Ben. He was no Bing Crosby and he had no wish to be. He wanted to sing in opera. He was very determined. I wanted to write and he wanted to sing. And we both wanted it so badly that it was certain we both would succeed. Not financially perhaps, but self satisfactorily.

At Toynbee Hall he made his mark in local amateur operatic performances. And at home he now sang in full voice, melodically, lyrically, pleasingly.

He could sing "Brown Bird" better than any voice I ever heard. When he sang this song I always wanted to cry. He sang it with such feeling, such thrilling sensitivity, such warmth, such pathos, such poignancy. He sang it for me, so that my heart opened to its trills.

He went on singing. He sang at concerts. He sang at parties. Bidden and unbidden he sang. He loved the sound of his own voice . . . and everyone who heard it loved it too.

His voice had developed into a *bel canto* — a true *bel canto*, sung from his deep chest and not tricked into a flash false note from the head. Singing with Tauber, the great Tauber, Ben could, at the final note, outmatch him and produce a true chest note when even Tauber had to resort to a head note, falsetto, thin.

His *bel canto* singing had a unique quality. Not once the times when the church castrated choirboys to keep them in such clear youthful voice all the days of their emasculated lives had a voice of this quality been heard. People who mattered began to take an interest in it. The radio, answering a question as to who had sung the highest note ever recorded, played a record that Ben had made from an aria by Bellini who wrote for *tenori castrati.*

Yes. He made records. Like my books they never sold. His efforts were for the connoisseurs, the cognoscenti, the specialists. He made records under the name of Benvenuti Finelli and collectors the world over sent for them; but here, in this country, no one bought them as no one bought my books. No one? Well, not in sufficient quantity to make it easy to live, he by his singing or me by my writing.

He sang the lead for one of the principal opera houses in the country. He went on tour with them. But he could always earn more by his trade of travelling and selling than by selling his voice. So he went back on the road.

I like to think of him as a strolling vagabond, as a wandering Orpheus making music on his rounds. He was born too late. In the Middle Ages Ben would have gone from castle to castle singing his lays, the troubadour to whom every drawbridge would have been run down in greeting.

I like to think of him walking the narrow wood lanes wild singing his songs . . . singing of the brown bird in dusky woods at twilight.

He sang on radio. He appeared later on television. He was always a success, but refused to chase it. He was offered the lead in a musical comedy. But it wasn't his kind of singing.

Now, singing not only in Italian but in Neapolitan, he sang Sorrento and Cateri here, years before they became popular. He made himself a corner in Neapolitan folk music and dipped into it to bring out rare musical treasures.

Of course, he could have made money by singing. There were two things against that. One was that he never needed to sing to eat. He always held down a good job. It would have been better in this respect if he had been the artist in the garret. But he could never see himself sacrificing what he already had, which was comfortable, for what could be, which might be fabulous. He played it safe. And in safety success never lies.

The second was that he would not indulge in prostitution. He could have been the greatest ballad singer of this or any other age, and many famous singers themselves, many impressarios, have said it. But he wanted to sing what he wanted to sing, not what the public wanted.

As for me, I shall never grow out of Brown Bird.

Down in the woods there's a little brown bird singing,
Singing in the hush of the darkness and the dew,
Singing in the hush of the darkness and the dew,
Oh but I wish that my thoughts could go a-winging,
Could go a-winging to you,
To you.

There was another song Ben discovered that, as soon as I heard it, enraptured me. On the reverse side, flip side as they say these days, of a pre-electric recording of Caruso singing a hackneyed song, "Because" by d'Hardelot, I think, was a song called "My Message".

It was a lyrical piece of emotional singing that enchanted me.

I sent you red roses and I know
My heart went with them when I
saw them go;
They carried in their petals love
for you —
And yet . . . who sent the flowers?
You never knew.

Perchance the flowers I sent you now
are dead,
Their message and their meaning
both are fled —
And though my soul went in their
leaves to you,
You never cared, sweetheart . . .
You never knew.

Maybe I was at a stage when, hungry for beauty and searching for lyricism, I went overboard for the sentimental. But the music had a strange haunting melody that made me surrender to it. Like poetry that sang, music that touched my heart overpowered me. I gave myself up to its poignancy and wallowed in tears. That's why I loved Joseph Kauffman of whom I shall tell you more later.

The years have not killed my tender soul. I am full of sighings when violins sing. And still when I hear Brown Bird I feel my brother Ben close to me and we are boys together treading the path towards the happy uplands.

He sang of the brown bird in quiet woods at eventide, singing enchantingly, melodiously, sweetly in haunting, measured cadences of pure delight. He sang of a brown bird in the woods and all the world lit up with new glories and summer stole into the sky and the wind and the stars were in my hair and peace lay in my heart.

Down in the woods there's a little brown bird singing — O, my heart! How it sings to the melody and the words. How it lives again those old happy far-off days.

Sing on, brother Ben, friend of my early years. Sing on. We who know you will treasure the echoes of your songs in our hearts till the last syllable of recorded time.

Why have the years come between us? Where are the twin joys we knew and the moments we both shared? What has time done to us, O friend and more than brother, flesh of my flesh and Jonathan to my David?

Lost and by-the-years-forgotten friendship return and make music that sings to us of days that will never be again.

For today is yet another day that is passing and all todays are wild with regret and weeping . . .

23

Born with "Braims"

TO prove that nothing succeeds like excess, as Oscar Wilde has said, I must tell you the story of David Dunks. He follows here by association with brother Ben who started life with nothing, while David began with everything in his favour.

When I entered Davenant as a twelve-year-old, David was in the fifth form, a tall big-nosed lad of sixteen, about to take his matriculation examination.

He was the son of wealthy parents. Under the name of Sleef there were three cafés in the Whitechapel Road and a fourth under the name of one of David's sisters. All the shops sold fashion. And since the Jewish girl of those days considered herself a fashion-setter and was infinitely better and more expensively dressed, albeit a shade more flashily, than her Gentile sister, the Sleef shops were in the money. They even had a chauffeur-driven car. In those days that was being a millionaire. Money they had in abundance. Brains in a *misère* of worthlessness.

When I reached the fifth form David was taking matric for the tenth time. He was then twenty, a man of a boy among us fifteen-and sixteen-year-olds, but friendly, charming, and of course always able to lay on parties and treats that to our starved eyes and stomachs were like Lord Mayors' banquets.

Yet he didn't buy popularity. We liked him. He was a big simple soul without malice or deceit in his make-up. Decent but stupid.

However, by dint of slogging and much coaching, bought at high expense, and experience gained from familiarity with the type of questions set, David got through at last.

His father, a shrewd little man who had made the Sleef fortunes, was happier than if he had opened another ten shops. He threw a big party. There, in his rooms over one of his cafés in the Whitechapel Road, he had about a hundred people.

Wine flowed like water. For the first time in my life I tasted caviare and champagne.

Old man Dunks made a round of his guests, his perky little face beaming with parental pride and joy. And, reaching me, he slapped me on the back and exclaimed: "I told you mine son had it braims like you got. I told you he tooks after me, I told you he had it braims after all."

To have "braims" — that was the ambition of all fathers for their sons, even when the fathers were so well breeched that their sons really didn't need "braims", to make their way in the world. But the Jewish tradition of learning died hard. Money did not make you a gentleman. Brains did. By this reckoning some of the boys who were boys with me should by now have found themselves in Debretts or Burke's Peerage. They haven't yet. The aristocracy of the Intelligence may be a far, far better method of class segregation than titles founded by illegitimate courtiers out of rompworthy courtesans, but the English will never have it so.

The boy David went on to hospital to study for a degree in medicine. Money in those days could secure entrance to a medical school. David took nine years to qualify. There were rumours of his being turfed out time and again; but the old man had a seat on the Board of that hospital and a few hundred guineas towards the hospital upkeep was worth, I suppose, the keeping of a student on course.

Another party. Nine years to finish a five years' course. Some going. David was now twenty-nine. He still had to walk the wards, do his prescribed course of internee work.

But, at something over thirty, David was almost ready to branch out as a fully-fledged doctor.

The old man brought him a big practice in North London. In no time at all David was the successful G.P. His patients believed in him, loved his charm, had faith in his ability.

How are patients to know if a doctor is stupid or not? He is a doctor, that's all. What do they care about his difficulties in passing examinations, provided that he can prescribe aspirin or castor oil when he knows what they are suffering from, or send them off to hospital when he does not know?

For that, as David himself told me, sitting in his luxurious surgery in the comfort of a deep leather armchair against a beautiful desk of tremendous size and smoking Corona Coronas (he offered me one, too), was the secret of his success. He prescribed only when they had colds or chills or influenza or — to him — easily recognizable, ailments. When he was unsure he never took a chance. Off to hospital. That, and a bedside manner, was all the G.P. needed.

Shades of Arthur Bromberg who went from Davenant to top the whole of England in anatomy and physiology and then, pressed to stay on to concentrate on research, reluctantly refused because he had to earn money quickly to support his parents. And, irony of ironies, both Bromberg's parents dying within six months of his setting up as a G.P. so that for many years afterwards he sighed for the scholarship which might have been his and the important work he could really have done. But Bromberg did well as a G.P. because of his almost uncanny rightness in the sphere of diagnostics. He could look at a patient and know what was wrong. His patients learned to trust his judgement.

Bromberg got there by brilliance. Bromberg, who had taken scholarships in History, Geography, Latin and Economics just to help pay his way through medical school and had never needed or wanted to use those subjects, got there the hard way, by brilliance.

David got there by charm. And money, of course. Without the help of L-s-d he would never have started. But, once started, he went merrily along. His patients loved his charm. He joked with them. He refused to take their complaints seriously. He actually made some of them better by his applied psychology. Bromberg cured them with knowledge. David with a laugh.

And yet there must have been more to it than that. For David was a good doctor inasmuch as his patients had faith in him. The charm that had made him a likeable lad made him, too, a sound physician. In my fulminating against the easy road that money can point to, I know I overlook the fact that in most cases a little more is needed. David did well because he *had* something, even if it was not native intelligence.

And David expanded his practice till it was so large that he had five assistants working under him and could sit back and relax. By the time he was forty David had to all intents and purposes retired. Bromberg retired too. To take up research. He had enough to live on if he went carefully. David bought himself a Rolls, with chauffeur, and a Bentley he drove himself. And a country house set in its own grounds.

Today, as I write, Bromberg is sweating away in the dim laboratory of a famous hospital, working to find a cure for the disease that killed both his parents — cancer. David is in the South of France where he spends four months in every year. Who is enjoying life the more? My guess is Bromberg. But David would argue this like mad.

At that first party I talked with his younger sister, Heather, a country-faced wench of good carriage and happy disposition. I think I lost my heart a little to Heather. Whatever it was I felt for her, it was absolute purity. Desire was not under the elms in those days of my life. The girl I wanted had to be purer than driven snow. And this Heather undoubtedly was.

I began to coach her for her matriculation. It was one way of getting close to her. She was almost as stupid as her big brother. Not quite. No one could have been that stupid. But there was a strong family resemblance. They were both very nice, charming people, too.

And sometimes I offered to walk with her. But why did Heather need to walk when the chauffeur would take her wherever she felt like going? I went for a ride with her once, my first ride ever in a chauffeur-driven car. It was nice to feel the closeness of her, to catch the scent of her fine, fair hair, to see those full red lips in their meeting and parting as they made words.

I was sixteen. She was fifteen. We were in love. We could tell this to one another and we did. Without a caress, without a kiss, we sighed out our love in an eye-searching purity of devotion. At this distance I know it was love and that she seemed afar and remote and so much my vision of the perfect female in life form.

But more and more she went out to parties and less and less I saw her. And slowly I faded out of the picture, cherishing the futility of it all to my secret soul and revelling in my unhappiness. This was Life (with a capital L, of course) as it had to be.

Many years later when I was visiting David she came into the room and I did not recognize her. The well-built girl had become the plump matron. Her fair hair had been dyed so many different shades that it was as wispy as sick corn and just as brownly yellow. The marks of good living were all about her — three chins, ample bosom fighting a losing battle against drag despite the artificial aids of modern uplifting, ponderous hips, swollen legs in absurdly tight little shoes that only made the ankles look even more ridiculous, no waist, puffed out cheeks, diamonds dripping on all fingers, neck swathed in furs — a made-up masquerade of beauty.

She had with her two awful children — a stuck-up snob of a boy just down from his expensive public school and a precocious little brat of a girl.

I thanked whatever gods may be for allowing me to suffer at sixteen all the pangs of unrequited love so that, at forty, I could look upon her not only with disenamoured but with disgusted eyes.

And yet I had once loved her with all the force of a schoolboyish passion. Then she was perfect. Was it more than disenchantment that let me see her as I saw her? Or was it sour grapes, too?

It is far better to have loved and lost than never to have loved at all. Wise old bird, Tennyson.

Have I been unfair to David? But then that old sour woodpecker that picks at my shoulder must be blamed. If there is an aristocracy of character (as I myself believe) then David is a king. And money or no money his kind of man would have gone a long way. Perhaps it is my own sourness that embitters me. My small talent might have been completely extinguished and not kindled by having had a rich father.

I am what I am and David is what he is in spite of the things we did or did not have. And I suspect he is a better man than I.

24

Imperishable Talent

THE boys who were boys when I was a boy go marching along with me. Rank on rank of shining faces. Boys of all shapes, sorts, sizes and not a nasty one in the whole bunch. Not a real wicked one. Most of them strugglers and stragglers along life's highway. Few of them favoured with the Sleef background; not one of them envious, as I was, of those who were richer.

Bageot became one of our leading architects. Harry startled blasé Fleet Street with many a piece of brilliantly written copy and a series of readable, impressive Leaders. Hyman achieved distinction in accounting circles. Shorty became an actor.

And there were others. Round-faced Manny Goodsmith, not one of the superlatively bright pupils but a good worker and always around the top half of the middle of the form, went on to make a name for himself as a writer of science for the masses and became scientific adviser to the United Nations. One of the finest Q.C.s of today was, as I remember, a nice enough youngster but something of a mediocrity in a school where brilliance abounded. One of the country's leading psychiatrists was one of our bright boys, though not the brightest, and there are at least two Members of Parliament who owe allegiance to my old school. There were also many nondescript and not a few failures. One tends to remember only the successes.

Such a one was David Sketcher (I shall call him) who went on to make a great name for himself as a cartoonist. Round-eyed, black-haired, handsome David, quite the best-looking youngster I ever saw, who managed to retain his good looks into middle age and develop his talent, obvious even then, to heights of fame.

There was also Henry Klutzak, another artist, a boy hopeless at school work but an angel with a brush. At sixteen Henry had two pictures hung in the Royal

Academy. They were views from his window over the teeming back streets of the East End. Views that did not miss a single cement seam or a flake on a wall. Views that were so meticulously precise in detail, so exact in out-of-focus clarity of vision that it was said he must have painted them looking through field glasses. And he did. Every lavatory seat in every scruffy back alleyway could be seen flat or upturned. Every leaking backyard pipe with every drop of water dripping from it. Every window, with the room beyond, or shielded by tattered curtains from prying eyes such as his.

Sixteen, and the critics went mad about him. The newspapers gave him front page importance. He was interviewed. Photographed. Lionized. Not one, but two pictures in the Academy. He became the rave of the artistic world.

Our Art Master, Black, who had himself won some small distinction with a series of posters for the then London transport board, was beside himself with glee. His big beard quivered with delight. One of his pupils could really paint.

But further fame eluded Henry. When

he left school he went on to draw nudes. Always a little eccentric, he took up a plane when we were retreating in France, took it up without orders, and fought the Hun in the sky till he ran out of fuel and crashed to smithereens. He shot down four enemy planes in the air and destroyed almost an entire column of marching Jerries as he crashed, deliberately perhaps, into their ranks and blew himself to final extinction.

Who, but those who knew him well, remembers Henry? And his effervescent talent and his loud, gruff way of speaking, and his argumentative manner that concealed a soft heart, and his shock of unruly hair falling about his face, and the way he used to plague and torture the teaching staff with deliberate mistakes in class and careless untidy blot-besmirched work. Henry, who could work to pin-point neatness on canvas yet couldn't write two words without smudging and dirtying a page. Lovable Henry — who remembers him now? Gone as if he never was. And those two brilliant canvases? Where do they hang and what tale do they tell their fortunate owners who do not, I presume, have to live in that clarity of poverty that Henry made beautiful and poetic?

Cleverness in class is not always the route to future success. Nor was it, remember, in the case of Churchill. A man needs more than scholastic ability if he is to make his mark. And if he has what it takes he won't need money to help him make the grade.

Many of those who could not pass examinations went into business and fared much better, financially speaking, than the clever ones. And even in scholarship, some of the early duds outpaced the top-of-the-class regulars. Late development? Not always. Luck followed some around, forsook others. It wasn't money alone that made the difference.

Smelinsky was a case in point. Smelly, we called him. And how he smelled. His clothes were shiny with age and dirt. His frayed cuffs gleamed from long wiping of his nose. His shirt was black with sweat and grime. He never washed. Slept in his clothes in a back room shared with eight brothers and sisters. Ate black bread sandwiches, dry, for his lunch. And was the biggest dud in the class, bar one — and that one, Sleef.

No one would sit with him. He sat at the back by himself near an open window. Time after time he was sent home to wash and returned as dirty and evil-smelling as ever. Teachers gave him up, refused to handle his books or think about him though, on hot afternoons, this last was impossible.

Smelly had actually won a Junior County Scholarship. Taking him without interviewing him (for he was conveniently sick every time they asked him to present himself) the school found that they had on their lists a boy they just couldn't get rid of. Health and Welfare visitors could do nothing for the Smelinsky *ménage*. The father was a biblical scholar who refused to work. Kind neighbours kept the family alive.

We would periodically club together at school to buy Smelly new clothes. The staff was always only too glad to contribute. With a new suit, clean shirt, tie free from soup and other stains, and boots that were whole and shiny, Smelly still smelled. The stink was indigenous. We never managed to cure it. And as for the clothes, they stayed bright for a week or so and then reverted to type.

Smelly got Matriculation much to everyone's amazement. Better boys than he failed. How did he do it? By sitting up all night, night after night, memorizing his work. Late developer, my foot. He was just a parrot who kept on repeating facts and figures to himself until some of them stuck.

And, wonder of wonders, Smelly was even accepted at a college. We bought him a new outfit for the occasion and he was taken on by Birkbeck. Three years after his matric, before some of us had passed our Highers, Smelly had qualified as an LL.B. Tonmais Smelinsky, Bachelor of Law.

No late development this. Sheer grind, sheer unadulterated slogging, sheer agony of work and toil and sweat . . . and smell? No, that's unkind. For when I next saw Smelly he was neat and tidily dressed and the smell had disappeared.

Smelly, before he was twenty, was actually keeping eleven souls — his parents, his eight brothers and sisters and himself — on what he earned as a cub solicitor.

Ten years after this and the Smelly I met was a real Edwardian dandy from the tip of his goatee beard to his neat burnished shoes. With carnation in buttonhole and goldmounted stick and his Homburg set over on one side and his nonchalant swagger he looked, and was, the real man about town. He had a flourishing law practice, had invested wisely in property and was wealthy. He was living in a flat in Curzon Street. I had a drink of sherry there. It was furnished in the grand manner with period pieces, and the tapestries and draperies were magnificent. And his wife turned out to be a bewitching creature whose fame as both a beauty and the daughter of a very wealthy father had often steered her into the Society columns of the better-class newspapers and magazines.

Smelly. Stinky. It was incredible. All done by late developing? Never. But you must take off your hat to Smelly. How he worked. How he burnt up those books. How he went short of food and sleep and even the barest comforts to get out of the smells and into the fresh air.

Smelly was making money, real money, whilst most of us were still sweating our way through college and telling ourselves what a hard life it was being a student son of poor parents.

I never plucked up courage enough to ask him why he had to smell when he was a boy. Maybe he had a good reason for it. Or whether the transformation had been slow or sudden. And when it was he decided that in hard work and not brilliance lay the seeds of success. For while the examination system flourishes so long will sheer determination and book swotting beat natural talent and ability. As my mother was always telling me: *A viller is besser den a kenner* which can be translated as: *He who wants to is better than he who knows how to.*

Hail Smelly and all the *villers*, the want-tos of this world. How you disprove the bitterness that tries to attribute success to a good start in life. These boys began with nothing, from nothing, and went on to conquer their worlds.

One with natural talent, supreme

natural talent and immense ability was Joseph Kauffman. A pale little boy with a shock of fair hair and a shy, quiet, likeable manner, Joseph was only just good enough in class to keep the teachers happy. But in the field of music he was magnificent.

He had been playing the violin since he was seven and at the age of twelve, when I first got to know him, was already giving recitals.

His father doted on him. There were no others. His mother was dead. His father was a tailor's presser, as my father had been — another scholar turned presser who sacrificed his health and comfort to give his son everything that had been denied him, the father. Mr. Kauffman, unlike old man Smelinsky who relied on the generosity of neighbours to keep him alive, kept himself alive by doing work for which he was not fitted by temperament or physique. As in my father's case, the strain was telling. Kauffman was older than he should have been at his age and weaker.

Yet the idea that his son would be a great violinist drove him. Lessons for

Joseph cost a great deal of money. So did a good instrument. But the money was found. By dint of hard work at the hot iron.

We used to visit Joseph — Hyman, Shorty, Harry, Jim, I and others — in the two rooms they rented off the Commercial Road: two rooms that Mr. Kauffman kept as neat and tidy as any good housewife might; and while we sat around on the floor and listened to Joseph play, he would make us Russian tea, strong tea served in tumblers, minus milk but with a slice of lemon added for flavouring.

And Joseph would play. Ah, those wonderful nights of music under East End skies. Ah, the heart-throbbing melancholy and the wistful melodic mournfulness of those wonderful evenings, the music, the togetherness, the enfolding aura of oneness, the silence, lovely music rising, swelling, taking possession of us, a room, five or six lads of twelve or thirteen, a throbbing violin and the old man crying quietly with joy and wonder and sorrow and pride.

Where today's boys are kicking their

heels to jungle rhythms and finding a beat, we learned, by listening, the worth and spiritual value of good music. What did it matter whether we understood what we heard or not? The point was that we *felt* it so deeply that nearly all of us found it hard to stifle tears. What is there about great happiness that brings the tears falling? For old man Kauffman was very happy those days and he cried very much. But perhaps the true-blue Englishman does not understand this.

When he was thirteen Joseph gave his biggest recital yet at the old Queen's Hall. The school turned up in force — there were about two hundred boys there and every one of the staff.

The hall was full. The East End knew about Joseph and was there to encourage him.

It was a memorable demonstration by a boy prodigy. Sometimes at night I wake up and I am back in that vast, wonderful hall and the music is all around me wrapping me in beauty and the last long note is drawn from the bow and there is a second's shattering silence and then the applause starts like an explosion and mounts like thunder till I see only hands, hands, hands, enthusiastically according a triumph and through those hands the pale face of Joseph smiling and the paler face of his father laughing while the tears stream from his eyes.

The critics raved about Joseph. Kreisler said, and I quote the words that I shall never forget till the end of my days: "This is the greatest living talent the world has seen." Yes, Kreisler said that.

The critics were almost as kind. Not one harsh word marred their enthusiastic eulogies. Joseph made the front page. He was news. At school we now had two heroes, Henry Klutzak the painter and Joseph Kauffman the musician. Two artists.

Mr. Kauffman now acted very wisely. He refused to be tempted by concert offers. Joseph must finish his schooling. When you think of the years of sacrifice Mr. Kauffman had nobly endured you will know how great must have been the temptation to take Joseph away from school and send him concert-touring round the world. America wanted Joseph. France begged for him. Scandinavia could arrange a series of concerts. Kauffman could have signed Joseph up for a world tour and gone with him and let the money roll into his lap. How many fathers could have resisted such temptation?

Old and weak and ill he was. But Kauffman was a man of high integrity. He was being true to his son. His whole life had been given to making his son a great success and what then did his own life matter? His son was not quite ready. In two or three years he would be that much better, finer, more capable musician.

Joseph dropped out of the news. He gave occasional concerts but not for money. He played for charity, he played at parties, he played for impresarios and for visiting musicians who wanted to hear this superb talent.

One day the great, lovable Ashermaun (I shall call him) was in England — Ashermaun, one of the fabulous names of violin virtuosity. And he it was who came to see the Kauffmans, and it was my great good fortune to be there.

Ashermaun who had played with

Caruso, for the Czar, in all the wonderful places of the world, before famous people in famous places. Ashermaun, who was already a legend. A round cuddly, teddy-bear of a man. A very human person. A typical Jew who felt inwardly and laughed outwardly and whose deep good nature filled you with a sense of warmth.

He had heard of the fame of Joseph. And he, the already famous, wanted to hear the famous-to-be.

Ashermaun the majestic and little Joseph. The Emperor and Joseph the dreamer.

And Joseph played Hebrew Melody, one of the maestro's own favourite pieces. A piece that cries aloud with all the tragedies and sufferings of this People. Poignant, moving, washed with tears and infinitely grand and inspiring.

And Joseph played.

And as he played, Ashermaun wept.

He, the master of the violin, weeping for joy and delight at the incomparable tone of the young Kauffman; weeping for the skill, the artistry, the executant ability and for the music, too. Weeping not only for the boy but for his People and for music. For music too.

In an excitement of living hundreds of days this one ineffable hour stands out glittering and golden, refulgent with brilliance and glowing brighter and brighter with each passing year. O this unforgettable hour. Time does not dim, it polishes the memory. It shines out of my love of living with unforgettable splendour.

Kauffman and Ashermaun embraced with tears. Both men were too full of inner ecstasy to speak. Words had no part in, could not utter what they were both feeling. The moment was too big for words. Too deep for anything but emotion. A moment made eternity.

I was crying, too. Crying unashamedly. Only Joseph smiled. It was as if he could stand apart from the overpoweringly moving music he made. Like a mathematical genius he could charm the notation into producing all the right answers and be unaffected by the result. He was Heifetz-like in his musical objectivity. He was detached — above and beyond mortal reactions. It was almost as if he fancied himself God.

When I remember now how I used to think *that* as a boy, seeing as a child in the clear limpid streams of thought in which a child sees, I am amazed that I was so near the truth. Then it was but an idea: *He thinks he is God*. And I dismissed it as a boyish criticism. Today I see it was the hub, the core, the systole and diastole of all that was to be. With immature eyes I had stumbled on a great truth. But only now do I see it clearly. Too late. Much, much too late.

For, by the time he was sixteen, Joseph did not think — he knew — he was God. He suddenly began to give commands and, if they were not obeyed, became violent. He attacked a teacher in school. He quarrelled violently with his friends. We all knew something was wrong. He spoke to us as if we were dirt. He talked down to us. He riled us. And till we understood that something was wrong with him we just sat on him, literally I mean, and he screamed like a demented woman till one of the masters came into the room and that was when he attacked this man, Mr. Robinson, going for him with a loose desk lid. Joseph might have broken the teacher's skull if we had not pulled our raving colleague away.

He was sent home. Everyone understood then that the sweet-natured, mild little Joseph was not himself.

But one night at home he attacked his aged father and only the neighbours, breaking down the locked door, saved Mr. Kauffman's life.

Joseph was declared insane and sent to a mental asylum in Surrey.

As soon as Mr. Kauffman was out of hospital he went to see him. But by that time Joseph did not recognize his father. He recognized no one. He had shut himself tight away in another world, in a world where he didn't even know or want to know a note of music. For the fiddle by his bedside stood dusty and unused. He never even looked at it.

They brought the greatest doctors in the world to see him, neurologists, psychiatrists, famous men of medicine. Every penny Mr. Kauffman had went on doctors. They pronounced schizophrenia, shook their heads and went away.

Every known form of treatment was tried including the then new electric-shock treatment. Joseph did not respond. He sat alone in his room, dejected, solitary, brooding. On what? God knows.

One day his father begged him, crying aloud on blended knees, to play. Joseph appeared to respond. Before a gathering of doctors and one of the masters at school, Mr. Banks, the music master who loved Joseph like a son, Kauffman's entreaties seemed to awaken some response.

Joseph went to the fiddle, dusted it down, tuned it and suddenly burst into the Devil's Trill by Tartini, a difficult piece even for acknowledged masters of the instrument. Without rehearsing, without seeing the score, without preparation, though his fingers were unsupple and he unpractised, he began to play perfectly, superbly, with that colossal arrogance and detachment that gave him such unparalleled and astonishing brilliance and perfection.

When everybody in the room was

crying he suddenly stopped in the middle of a note, laughed madly, broke the violin across his thigh and flung the pieces into his father's face.

The old man collapsed on the spot. He never recovered from the stroke. Three days later he was dead.

Joseph lingered on for four years. We, his erstwhile friends, used to go and see him near the end. He had grown fat and bestial. He slobbered. He was dirty. He sat there, a mountain of flesh, and never even looked at us as we entered his room in company with a male nurse, never even lifted his head to stop brooding. He sat there, head down, gazing intently at the wooden blocks on the floor. Suddenly he would wet himself and never even change countenance.

It was horrible.

Dementia praecox had set in. His actual brain tissue was degenerating.

And then one day we heard he had died. He was not yet eighteen.

He left behind him an imperishable memory of sublime music — but only in the minds of those who were privileged to hear him play; and two records, both of which I value more highly than all the perfume of Arabia, all the wealth of Elman, of Menuhin and Heifetz, the Oistrachs and yes, even Ashermaun.

If I told you his real name you might know it. Lovers of music would. He was destined to be one of the world's greatest violinists, one of the greatest of all time, and he was dead before he was eighteen.

Do you care? I care. I care, I care, I care, I care, I care. God how I care. Who else is left to care or remember?

Those whom the gods love. How they must have worshipped this sweet, innocent, kindly lad to change him thus into a monster.

By what valleys and deep slumbering streams do you play now, O Joseph? For whom do you make your divine music? Or is your genius forever silenced, dead for all time, lost and gone?

O life that turns young hearts to stone. O living that changes boys to beasts and brilliance to madness and hope to despair. Shall we see again this talent awaken, catch the mountain notes wild across the world? Shall we hear again the sweet inexpressibly sad songs he made? Shall we walk with him again in boyhood's dreams?

Are you there, Joseph, on the far-off hills?

25

Swot Shop

BUT of course there were days when Joseph was just a boy. When we were all just boys of fifteen, sixteen and seventeen, just growing up.

When school was over for the day we gathered in the Whitechapel Library. It was our meeting-place, our club, our *alma mater.*

I would play football in the large, almost full-size football pitch playground attached to Davenant, walk home, have tea, listen to Jack Payne, Jack Hylton, Joe Loss, Roy Fox or one of the other popular dance bands that used to play regularly at that hour at that time at that day and age, then gather up my books and go off to the Reference Library and Reading Room of the Whitechapel Library. The Swot Shop, as we called it.

It was a large room on the first floor, furnished with long straight tables, chairs, good lighting, a counter at which you could refer to a long list of books and have them sent up for your inspection and temporary perusing, and, most important of all, a host of good friends and companions met there nightly to pretend to work.

At the Bethnal Green Library there were individual desks for swotters. At the Mile End Library there was a better service of reference books and more decorum. The real workers, the swots and studiously bent, might go to Bethnal Green or Mile End. But for a lark there was no place to beat Whitechapel.

Here I would find Hyman, Jim, Harry, Shorty, Bageot, Judah Cohen-called-Kern, Bernie, Manny, Henry Klutzak, Sketcher, Smelly (a discreet interval of space between him and the next boy), Joseph Kauffman (when he could spare the time from music and before he went mad), David Dunks accompanied by his sister Heather, Arthur Bromberg, a boy called Bedlowsky (whom we called Bedhigh) and most of my school friends and classmates.

The neighbouring, rival school, the

Central Foundation School, at which my brothers Edward and Mark had been pupils and the girls' section which my sister Betty attended, also supplied a quota of students. They were far more serious than we. We laughed at them as swots. But they produced almost as many famous men as our school did, their now leading light being a very learned professor of television and Brains Trust fame.

Why did we go to the Whitechapel Library? Not to work — though our homework did get done, somehow or other. No. It was because we did not have facilities at our homes for quiet working, no room, no space, hardly a clear table on which to set out our books. The Library offered us free space, warmth, light and, of course, merry companionship.

We were not supposed to talk. A short, dark thick-set young man whom everybody detested, would shout "Quiet! Quiet, please!" if the talking grew audible; and then, if it did not stop, would come across and ask you to leave.

Once when Shelton and Dunks were roaring over some joke, Old Toughegg, as we dubbed him, demanded that Dunks get up and go. Dunks was not used to being spoken to like that. He was almost as old as Toughegg anyway. He refused to budge.

Toughegg sent for the police. We watched Dunks being thrown out — the two cops had to lift him bodily and haul him out. Next day he was back, glaring malevolently at Toughegg, and Toughegg, deciding that enough bother had been caused, left him alone.

But some were barred the Library for a while. Bedhigh threw stink bombs around the place one night. This was the cue for everyone present to hold their nostrils, make loud sounds of disgust, laugh like mad under their breaths and explode at times into guffaws of boisterous laughter.

It was terribly funny, really. The place held about a hundred people and those who were not serious and sniffing were funny and sniffing. It was a huge joke. Uproar became pandemonium and Toughegg, poor fellow, had to do his duty.

Sniffing like a bloodhound he traced the bombs, picked up the shattered remnants of broken glass delicately between two outstretched fingers and deposited them somewhere outside. He returned with a beefy porter.

After much argument and investigation, the whole place in a mad riot of mirth and yelling, Toughegg pin-pointed Bedhigh, and his beefy accomplice made to grab him.

But Bedhigh was tall, well-built, athletic, and as the beefy one made to grab him, Bedhigh slipped from his chair and pushed it under the beefy one's leaning body so that he stumbled across it and fell over the desks, upsetting a couple of bottles of ink and spoiling a few decently kept homework books. One was a girl's. And she began to scream hysterically.

Then we had the sight of Toughegg and his porter chasing Bedhigh around the room, between the chairs, over the tables, under the tables, until we could not contain ourselves with laughter.

It was the police — four of them — who finally grabbed Bedhigh and hauled him out. He had to spend a night in a cell before being released. And, after that, he was barred admittance by the beefy porter who kept the gate as part of his official duties.

So, much to our wild amusement, Bedhigh disguised himself and came in one night wearing dark glasses and a false beard and stage moustache and walking as though he were a hunchback so that Mr. Beefy Porter had let him through.

Of course, as soon as we saw him come through the swing doors, we knew him. There was a wild concerted outburst of laughter that shook the roof.

Toughegg looked up, saw Bedhigh, couldn't recognize him, and let him sit down. He took his seat next to us in a long row. And the sight of his face in his crude disguise sent us into paroxysms of mirth. We rocked and rolled with laughter.

Toughegg, his dark brows beetling, came and stood over us and shouted at us to be quiet. But how could we be quiet? There was Bedhigh taking out a scholar's atlas and starting to work, and he was got up to look like an old man.

Toughegg stared at Bedhigh. There was something fishy here. A man with a beard did not produce an exercise book and school homework. But he couldn't fathom it. We watched him, watched Bedhigh and just could not stop laughing.

And when his beard fouled Harry's book and Harry immediately clapped his hands on it so that the elastic stretched and then, suddenly, let go so that the beard shot back into Bedhigh's jaw and he winced, with suitable audible accompaniment . . . when we fell off our chairs, doubled up in the agony of suppressed guffaws, Toughegg knew a game was being played on him.

He grabbed the false beard. Bedhigh backed, ducked suddenly, and beard and moustache went plummeting right into Toughegg's swarthy face. He darted forward to grab Bedhigh and Bageot put out a foot.

As Toughegg hit the floor everyone began yelling and throwing books and banging on the desks. It was just like a prison riot.

It took a whole force of police to stop that one. We were all cleared out. The Library was closed for the night.

Bedhigh was back next night, looking

like Bedlowsky, and was allowed in. Everything was quiet.

He was a lively lad, very popular, full of high spirits and quite bright, brilliant in fact at English. He could write more than well. I have before me now a faded yellow copy of the school magazine with an article by him entitled "The Jazz Trombonist in Hell" and it has adult merit and adult perception. He had a flow, a gift for word command, an understanding of English writing that spelt success.

But he was useless at French. In those days matriculation had to be passed in three main subjects — English, Maths and a Language, and two subsidiary subjects. Today it is easy. G.C.E. is given away almost for free. But then many a promising pupil failed because of weakness in just one subject.

Our compulsory language was French. And Bedhigh couldn't make rhyme or reason of it. Twice he took matric and failed twice. His parents were too poor to keep him at school and he was taken out and found work in a tailor's shop.

I used to see him carrying sacks of

cuttings on his back and I thought, then, what a waste of talent this was.

But Bedhigh was happy. He had no ambition. Today he still carries sacks of cuttings on his back. He is poor. But he is one of the most unambitious men I know. He sets no store at all by monetary possessions or fame. Which seems to make some sort of a point to the carping woodpecker on my shoulder.

Unlike Bernie, who left and went into a factory and became factory minded, Bedhigh has kept up his reading and his friendships. He talks well, intelligently. His three little rooms, off Bow Road, tidily kept by his wife who shares his views on life, receive many visitors. His old friends and new ones, doctors, lawyers, musicians, artists, even politicians, come there to find mental stimulation and good company.

No one plays cards. No drinks are handed round. Men and women sit on the floor with a cup of coffee at their sides and everybody has fun.

He has become the centre of a discussion group where the flow of talk is adult and alert. People look forward to dropping into Bed's place (today we've dropped the High) and talking the night away.

The following day Bed will be seen toting his bundles of cuttings through the City.

I have often asked him why he does not write. He just doesn't want to. He can't be bothered. "What for?" he says. "Money?" he says. "I don't want money. I'm not interested in having other people read what I write. I'm unambitious, if you like. But I like life this way . . . "

Which is why he has remained content to be a carrier. And since there are small firms in the East End who still use a personal carrier for their cuttings, Bed is always in work. I don't suppose he'd mind much if he weren't.

But to return to the Library. It was not only a place where one could just about get an hour's homework done in four hours, but a meeting-place for boys and girls. It was something like a drugstore without the coloured drinks.

The girls of many different schools sat there and the boys of other schools helped them with their homework. It was a nice way to start a beautiful friendship.

Then you walked the girl home. If she liked you and you liked her, you walked her home again the next night. You never started any funny business, for these girls were not that kind. Bageot refused to waste his time on them. But you could find a mate. Three marriages I know began as boy and girl romances in the Whitechapel Reference Library. And so they consummated their studyings . . .

Boys who worked really hard went home, after the Library had closed down for the night, and began to work then. Others, like me, considered we had worked enough. Bromberg, however, would start work at half past ten and work till one a.m. each morning. Hyman till midnight. Shorty ditto. Even Bageot worked well into the night.

There was a secrecy about this extra work. Boys liked to make believe and make others believe they did not swot. It was considered slightly *infra dig* to swot. Yet the bright ones, like Bromberg, who were determined to get ahead because their parents were struggling hard to keep them at school, and the not so bright who resented their low places in class, both burned the midnight oil. But you would never hear anyone saying he stayed awake working and studying. In fact boys would tell you quite blithely that they never worked. By not working you covered yourself against possible failure and became "one of the boys".

My school fellows never believed me when I told them I didn't work hard. They would grimace and wink and look at one another as if to say: *he comes top and he's trying to tell us he does it by not working hard.*

But it was true. I could, but wouldn't concentrate. I had no capacity for hard work. I either mastered a subject in class and, by virtue of a very good memory, recalled it at the right time, or was quick witted enough to think faster than most. But when in later years the subjects demanded a deeper study than a teacher could impart, when it was necessary to read and study deeply, I began to fall away. Superficial brightness will not keep you at the top of a form where the stolid, solid students are really slaving to master their subjects. I fell away badly and found the passing of examinations an ordeal.

For a long time I even refused to face the truth myself. But eventually I found it. I would not work hard. I liked learning to come easy. And when it didn't, I almost did a Bedhigh. I changed eventually. But only when the fact of having to earn a living taught me that you couldn't go through life shining with superficial brilliance without the shine stemming from some deep down natural gem of understanding that had to be dug and laboured and sweated for . . . and then polished to brightness with years of laborious grind.

Certainly at the Whitechapel Reference Library I never worked. I went to chat with friends, to try and "get off" (the then current phrase) with a girl and to have a laugh.

Isn't it peculiar how laughs are always more enjoyable in places where they are strictly forbidden?

It reminds me of the cartoon I saw once. It showed a notice board on a bare, deserted, shingly beach, that stretched for miles in a solitude of stoniness. On the notice board was written: "It is forbidden to throw stones at this board".

So with the Library. It was fun because so much was forbidden. Even quiet talking was forbidden. We used to get up to all sorts of capers, hiding books, taking coats from one peg and putting them on another at the far end of the room, putting pins on chairs (we who thought this sort of trick was below and beneath us at school considered it good enough for Library fun) and generally striving to find sources of merriment.

It was good, too, after sitting in the Library for a couple of hours to get up, stretch yourself, and wander out into the Whitechapel Road to buy a soft drink, smoke a fag, and savour the delight of a break from too much studying.

All that work. What a hard life it was.

And the bare lone trees in the churchyard of the Whitechapel Road looked down upon us and the grey clouds moved under a grey sky and we walked out of the Library, into it, out of it, into it and out again at night into the fashionable parade of the

Whitechapel Road where the girls strolled with all the aplomb and something of the elegance of females fatales in the Champs-Elysées. The Road, we called it. Up the Road. Down the Road. That's where you went when you were lonely. And there, physically lonely you might go on being, but your brain was soon peopled with crowded thought.

26

Gobby

LOOKING back over the years I feel that the man who had the major share in shaping me, who left a lasting impression, was "Gobby" Evans.

He was the English master at Davenant and, like so many good English masters before and since, he was a Welshman, finding in the roll of prose and the lilt of poetry that music for which his Gaelic soul craved.

I have forgotten, if I ever knew, his Christian name, except that the initial was R and maybe it stood for Rhys. But Gobby he was to those who liked him, and those who didn't, on account of the way he would spit through his ill-fitting false teeth when addressing the class.

A quiet man, he was. Short and dark, with pin-point brown eyes that were never still. Neat, tidy, precise both in speech and appearance. A pedant, without doubt. A lover of English without equal.

He maintained discipline quietly and effectively. There were those big men like German master Bandt who shouted and raved and could not keep a class still. There were the big lumbering loose-limbed fellows like Black, the Physics master, whom everybody loved yet of whom no one was afraid, so that even while the boys liked him, they could not respect him because he could not keep them in order.

Gobby was not liked by many. Boys who had difficulty in finding something to like in English, easiest of all languages to learn, most difficult of all to master, found Gobby not to their taste. But everyone respected him. In his class silence was the order of the day and work went on apace, apace, even when it didn't wear a lovely face.

I came under his spell when I was not quite twelve and remained under it until I was past eighteen. In those days, when I was an East End boy searching for beauty, hardly knowing what I was searching for, fighting against all sorts of bad beginnings and unrewarding examples, he more than anyone taught me to love our tremendous heritage of English language and literature.

He never ordered. He led. He would lend me books to read and then, afterwards, discuss them with me. He would bring to my notice some good piece of writing and ask me to commit it to memory because, even if I did not fully understand it then, I would appreciate it later. Invariably I did and later understood.

He encouraged me to write, even to write puerile poetry. He was the one person to whom I showed my scribblings, of whom I was never afraid, and to whom I could confide, in writing, my secret longings and desires. All, of course, but sex. We never discussed that. I never wrote about it. And we just forgot it existed. And quite honestly it did not exist in that world through which Gobby taught me to walk with open ears that listened eagerly to every word, every change in metre.

He read Ruskin with me. Carlyle. Macaulay. When the class was dismissed we would sit on reading chapters of one of his favourite books to one another. So that I began to love what he loved and my literary taste today, for what it is worth, is a pale reflection of Gobby's.

Like me — or am I now making the mistake of assuming that we shared a liking instead of my growing to share his? — he preferred the lyrical and sensuous in poetry to the staid prosy pieces that went their elegiac way in round, sonorous phrases.

He had a tongue for beauty. He could find music in line after line of poetry that, on first reading, seemed not to be overful of lilt or lyricism. Word imagery thrilled him. Onomatopoeia intrigued him. Assonance was music to his ear. Figures of speech were as lucid to him as mathematical formulae to the physicist. Always he could make wonderful singing be heard when he read and always I followed him, only too glad to find a kindred soul.

Shakespeare I swallowed in large, appetizing chunks. Delighted to find in me one who could memorize fast, he pushed stuff at me as fast as I could read. We sailed through all the plays, the sonnets; went on to Donne and Blake and Spenser and, as I grew older, we vied with one another to bring beauty in language to each other. I would discover a line, a verse, a poem and he would match it with a find he had made.

It was a two-way traffic. I first brought to his notice the lyrical prose outpourings of Thomas Wolfe — Wolfe the lush lover of words, that uneconomic wordsmith who threw his words together in a heap and out of the tangled mass of over-richness produced incomparable writing; Wolfe, my hero of the full, mad, poetic phrase; Wolfe, whose overblown ripeness of writing almost suffocates by the intensity of its dark beauty; Wolfe I brought, and Gobby loved him. And Saroyan; and Gobby liked him too. And Dos Passos, the early Hemingway and the later Steinbeck.

Music I heard with him was more than music and bread I broke with him was more than bread.

Then Browning. The Browning I could not fathom. Whose word music I could hear but not comprehend.

Hobbs hints blue,
Straight he turtle eats;
Nobbs prints blue,
Claret crowns his cup.
Nokes outdares Stokes in azure feats.
Both gorge.
Who fished the murex up?
What porridge had John Keats?

It was Gobby who made me see the sense and therefore the beauty in those lines. He it was who fished the murex up for me so that I could stare in wonderment at the blue Tyrhennian dye. He it was who taught me what was sham and worthless in poetry and language, so that the Hobbs and the Nobbs, the Nokes and the Stokes who were mere copyists began to lose favour in my sight.

Teacher, mentor, guide — all these Gobby was to me. As I grew to man's estate he became a friend rather than a teacher. He had a daughter of about my age and I like to think he looked upon me as a son. Certainly I thought of him as my father.

After I left school I saw him only once again. He had been made Headmaster and I came to congratulate him. An emotionless man on ordinary levels, one who (as I knew, perhaps I alone) steeled himself to face the day, and only in the unutterable loveliness of sublime poetry allowed himself to nod, he was, that day, as near tears as I'd ever seen him.

I had written once or twice before, and after that meeting I only wrote once again. But the meeting itself was memorable for all the things we felt but never said.

Perhaps I was too close to the time to know the tremendous effect Gobby had had on my living, the wonderful things he taught me that would never pass away while I drew breath. Perhaps I did not see then, as I see all too clearly now, that Gobby gave me beauty I could savour — I, who had looked for it vainly everywhere and, till coming under his spell, had never found. He gave me the part of me I like best in myself — there are so many parts I shy away from.

And yet I did not see him again between my twentieth year and his death some fifteen years later. I did not write to him even. I just let him pass out of my ken of living as though he were just another landmark on the way. I took him for granted as one tends to take teachers for granted as men just doing their jobs.

But when I heard he was dead I went away and my heart overflowed. Gobby Evans, lover of language, you old Welsh charmer. Gobby Evans — do you sing to the stars beneath a moon in paradise? Have you sung your sweet songs into the ear of God? Be sure He will listen to one who so loved beauty, who so fed beauty into the hands of those born into the unloveliness of that East End, who gave his life to that end. Gobby, dispenser of beauty.

Men are born. Men die. How many leave behind them something really worth while? In my heart and in the hearts of those who were captivated by his fanatical enthusiasm for the spoken word, Gobby sowed immortal seed. In turn I have passed this craving for beauty on to my daughter. She, no doubt, will see that it does not die. Thus has Gobby Evans achieved his everlastingness.

Small though he was, what a man of great stature he made himself. How richly, how magnificently he toiled to spread his gospel of beauty. And how nobly he succeeded.

And him I let go, let slip away as though he never had been. And now he is dead.

They told me Heraclitus,
They told me you were dead;
They brought me bitter news to
    hear
And bitter tears to shed
I wept as I remembered
How often you and I
Had tired the sun with talking
And sent it down the sky.

This was one of his favourites. Another was Henley's *Margueritae Sorori*:

A late lark twitters from the quiet
    sky,
And from the west, where the sun,
His day's work ended,
Lingers as in content,
There falls on the old grey city
An influence luminous and serene,
A shining peace.

.   .   .   .   .   .

The lark sings on.
The sun, closing his benediction,
Sinks, and the darkening air
Thrills with a sense of the triumphing
    night.
Night with her train of stars
And her great gift of sleep.

So be my passing.
My task accomplished and the long
    day done,
My wages taken and in my heart
Some late lark singing.
Let me be gathered to the quiet
    west,
The sundown splendid and serene
    Death.

I know when Gobby died some late lark sang. It will sing in my heart for the rest of my days and then perhaps in other hearts until the end of recorded time.

He loved and taught me Christina Rosetti's gem of a poem. Now I quote it back for him:

When I am dead, my dearest,
Sing no sad songs for me.
Plant thou no rosebush at my head
Or shady cypress tree.
Be the green grass above me,
With flowers and dewdrops wet,
And if thou wilt, remember,
And if thou wilt, forget.

If thou wilt, remember . . .

O Gobby, Gobby, how can I ever forget?

27

Oxford Schol.

IN my last year at Davenant, I got an Oxford Scholarship. It was a competitive examination open to the whole country. Only one scholarship was given. About a thousand pupils from Grammar and Public schools took the written papers in English Language and Literature.

Forms of application were sent me. I had to choose a college and apply for a grant and send the forms back.

My family was beside itself with delight. I was in heaven. All my life I had dreamed of getting to Oxford. To me it had been a beautiful day-dream. I never expected to see it materialize.

I arrived at Oxford for the interview. The dreaming spires confirmed my most fanciful impressions. This was a ghettosnipe's Paradise. A book of verses underneath the bough and my work beside me in this setting and all my dreams would come true. I wanted no more from life. I had come a long way. Out of the gutter to this abode of kings. From Goolden Street and Broughton Buildings to the Isis and wonderland.

I faced a long line of professors. They fired questions at me. I had not expected a *viva voce*. But I was getting one. And coming through. Few pupils of my age could have known the English language better or its writers and poets more familiarly than I. I had lived with words since I was seven. They fascinated me. As most boys play with toys so I played with words. I lisped in numbers for the numbers came.

When one of them threw at me a line from an obscure poet, I was able then (though I could not now) to continue the stanza to the end.

When they asked me the law relating to "one" and "none" and the usage of "may" and "might", I threw Sonnenschein, Fowler and Partridge at them.

It did me good to see them shake their heads and cluck their tongues approvingly.

Then they said: "Latin?"

"Latin?" I said. Davenant did not teach Latin until the Sixth. In the first year I had mugged through a five years' Latin course to take Latin as an extra subject after matriculation and only just scraped through. I was now working at it to try and pass my inter-B.A. I had no background in the subject. No depth. It was all superficial knowledge designed to help me pass exams. One had to have Latin to take an Arts degree. But I had never guessed that it was part of the open scholarship exam.

However, I muddled through. When they read me parts, I could not say who had written them. I was no judge of style. But I could translate and understand.

They shook their heads at my pronunciation. I said "*Veni, vidi, vici*", using the hard "V" and the soft "C". They said "weenee, weedee, weekee". It was terribly confusing.

I was getting annoyed, too. Hadn't I passed their lousy exam? What more did they want?

Then they said "Greek?" and my world collapsed. I knew no Greek. I shook my head in dumb amazement as they mouthed Greek at me.

"Don't you know *any* Greek?" one of them asked.

"None."

"Little Latin and less Greek." They repeated the hoary quip.

"'*Small* Latin and less Greek'; Johnson said 'small' not 'little'" I was quick to point out, glorying in the fact that I could correct those supercilious bastards.

But they came back at me with "None! But *you* know none."

"None?" The old jossers were incredulous.

"Don't they teach it in the East End?"

"They have no time for it," I said. I meant *no time* in actual measured periods of hours, weeks, days. They thought I meant *no use* for it. They didn't like what I said.

"Surely," one persisted, "you must know something."

"Rhododactulos eos," I said. I had seen the words once. Their rhythm had caught my poetic fancy.

"Yes?"

"Rosy-fingered dawn," I said. Lovely words.

"Write them . . . There, on that board . . . No, in Greek."

How did one write Greek? I proceeded to write, in my best calligraphy, a line of Hebrew.

"That's not Greek."

"It's Greek to you," I said. I was fed up. This was not at all what I had expected. Curiously enough, my retort raised a laugh.

One of them asked me what it was.

"Hebrew, Biblical Hebrew. Older and more beautiful than Greek."

Most of them had known. They were merely trying to see if I knew too.

"Translate, if you please."

I translated: "'In the beginning God created the heaven and the earth. And the earth was without form and void. And there was darkness upon the face of the earth. And God said, Let there be light, and there was light.'"

I read it too. "*Bahrayshees, borroh Elouheem ess hushomahyeem ve-ess hohoretz . . .* "

I declaimed it. I revelled in the familiar sounds.

They appeared to be suitably impressed.

324

But no Greek. No Greek. They clucked like a lot of old hens.

And then . . .

"Which college did you stipulate?"

I told them.

"How do you spell it?"

"H-a-r-f-o-r-d," I said.

"Would you be surprised to learn that there is no such college?"

"But I know someone there!"

"At Hertford (they spelt it out for me) perhaps. Not a very encouraging start is it for someone who is supposed to know the English language?"

How could I tell them? There was a manager at the boys' club I attended who went to "Hertford". He had told me it was cheaper than the popular colleges or the famous ones. Advised me to choose it. He said "Harford" and I, who didn't know the names of any colleges beyond Balliol, had written as he spoke.

They finally offered me a free place. They couldn't give me the top award with its scholarship grant but they would condescend to give me one of the lesser places without grant.

I accepted.

Aided by a School Leaving Scholarship and a Prize especially awarded at Davenant to "a pupil of outstanding merit", an award known as the Groves' Memorial Prize, I went up, spent one miserable term in my own company, not being able to afford to join any of the clubs, not even the Chess Society, found living intolerable and life unbearable and my meagre funds unable to pay for my books, and went back to London University.

It was for me the death of a dream.

And many years passed before I was able to live with my disappointment and my ruined hopes. Hey . . . get off my shoulder you flaming bird!

I did not even take my degree. It was the period of mass unemployment, the hungry thirties. To get out of college and into the world quickly I took a teaching certificate and spent a few years teaching in the dockside slums before some limited success at writing helped me to a job in Fleet Street and from there into advertising.

For a time I took all sorts of University Courses in English Language and Literature to bolster up my loss of letters; but after a time I just went on reading for the sheer joy it gave me and was content to be recognized in my job by my ability alone.

But O the lost dream and the lost world and the lost books of verses under lost boughs. And O the anguish and the hurt and the melancholy as the dream receded and stern reality and dockside slums and hungry children and dirty buildings and unloveliness and misery took over.

O my dream city of dreaming spires. And O the sad sad years of adjustment.

28

Neurosis

ALL my life I had been hyper-sensitive and I suppose slightly neurotic.

As a youngster I believed that if I missed the paving cracks or kicked something into the gutter or turned round three times God would reward me. And if I didn't He would punish me.

This is fairly common to all youngsters and much of it leaves them in later life, though more men and women than we imagine are always slightly infantile in this respect. Early neuroses don't go altogether. Hence superstition. Hence those who count everything and those who touch objects and those who do every little deed in an ordered way.

If you put your left shoe on first every morning you are not, as you tell yourself, doing something out of habit. It would worry you if you put your right shoe on first. You would have a bad day. You would think or your subconscious would think that God was going to punish you for doing the wrong thing. If it wasn't God it would be just a vague fear that somehow someone somewhere would punish you for putting the wrong shoe on in the morning or taking the wrong shoe off first, last thing at night.

All of us are to some extent or other ruled by unreasonable fears. None of us is one hundred per cent sane. There is no such thing as normality. The normal person, were he completely normal, would soon find himself shut up in a lunatic asylum. He would be out of step with the world.

Most of us manage to keep in step. We look at the gastaps and reassure ourselves that we are taking reasonable precautions to ensure that there is no leakage. We check our rail tickets three times over and convince ourselves that it is absolutely necessary to make sure we have not lost them. We turn back a page in the dictionary to look at a word that has caught our eye in the flipping through and escaped us, to tell ourselves that we are really keen to know what the word was. We count stairs going up and down; patterns on wallpaper. We read the end of a book first. We put our coins into a certain part of a certain side of our clothing. We prefer to walk on one side of the road; could not possibly live in a house on the wrong side of the street.

Creatures of habit? Maybe. But far more likely we are, with these little acts known only to ourselves, propitiating the unknown deity. We are all suffering in some form or another from a Guilt Complex or a God Complex or one of the many other complexes that the psychiatrists have given names to. We're all mad, thank God, in a mad world.

Bageot found that when he was first married he was impotent. He went out and bought a harlot and was as good as ever he had been. But, with his wife, he remained impotent. It was Bromberg who put him right; who told him he had a Guilt Complex. His inner conflict produced his outward hesitancy.

Bageot confessed to his wife, was railed at, forgiven and saw his spirit rise again. He promised to be true and was for a long time. But when he strayed again and was immediately reduced to fumbling impotency, his wife knew at once that he had been up to no good. Confessing his sin, he was cured.

Still again, many years later, he went off the rails. And immediately his wife knew. This time she left him for a while and came back to him only after he had sworn by the Holy Bible and his three children never to stray . . . not ever.

He has wanted to at times. It has been difficult not to. But he knows now that he cannot hide his infidelity. So he remains pure and true to the only woman he really loves.

"Of course I could have cured him," Bromberg told me. "It would have taken a long time, but I could have got him readjusted. But what was the point? Knowing him as I do, as you do, we know that he would have been off the rails at least twice a week. Better this way. He has to be faithful. His penis is his conscience — and don't you fall for that old one about it not having one. It has. In the deep recesses of the mind, it has. Roger's has, that's certain."

Like Bageot we are all conditioned by some form of guilt or complex.

As a youngster I had it worse than most. I was a twister, a turner, a toucher of posts, a counter. Later on, when I learned that Dr. Johnson could never pass a post without touching it, even crossing over to the other side of the street to give way to his compulsion, I found strength in the knowledge that I was not so peculiar after all.

For, for many years I did think that it was only I, I alone, who was being pulled hither and thither by the irresistible forces that made me do what I knew I really didn't want to do. In my case it was God who made me do these things. Blame that, if you like, on a deeply religious upbringing and some primitive injunctions by ignorant teachers of English or Hebrew to do as I was told or God would punish me.

I know my Zaida never threatened me thus. Mother certainly didn't. Somewhere along the line, however, the fear of God had been put into me. It can be a terrible thing in a young, imaginative mind.

Imagination, Carl Fallas says somewhere,

is the gift of God in a child. In an adolescent, verging towards manhood, it is the devil's own gift. Keats says much the same in that preface to *Endymion* with which I began this book.

And that was so true of me. For the older I grew, the more obsessed did I become with totem and taboo, hoodoo and voodoo. But it was hidden, it was controlled, it was secret from everybody else — except that my family would watch me inspecting gastaps and snigger a little.

"No harm will come to us," mother would say. But that wasn't the point. Harm would come to me, to me not to them, if I did not inspect and re-inspect and re-re-re-re-inspect the already securely turned off taps.

And then, in my college days, with unemployment so rife that everyone one met was out of work and I only six months away from an English Honours degree and, since I had by then learned to work hard, from a possible First (for which I was freely tipped), someone I met told me I was wasting my time. He, who had already got his degree and was taking another to waste time, was out of work; had gone back to college to add to his qualifications while times got better. He warned me that a degree was no use to me. *Get yourself a working qualification*, he urged.

Doing what?

I groped for an answer and found it. I would take a Teaching Certificate and get work. Teachers were still finding jobs here and there.

But a Teaching Course in those days lasted over two or three years. Could I do it? Possibly, if I took English as my Advanced Subject — there wouldn't, couldn't be a lot of work for me to do there — and History, Geography, Art, Education, Physical Training, and Handwork rather than Music as my subjects of study.

By pulling strings and putting my case before various College Principals, I was finally admitted to a Teaching Course. I had six months to complete it. Twelve weeks of that had to be spent in School Practice, actually teaching in various schools under the eyes of Board of Education examiners. That left me twelve weeks to complete a Three Year Course.

How I worked. I hardly slept. I paced the room memorizing large chunks of History and Geography books. I spent every waking minute of every day swotting like fury, working till three and four in the morning, getting up at seven, working till nine, and dashing off to college for lectures.

What was the toll? Because a toll had to be paid. Complete and utter nervous breakdown. Yet nobody knew. Not a soul was aware of what I was going through.

For as the examination drew nearer I found myself completely unable to resist any and every compulsion. On the way to college, for instance, the 'bus would pass a street and I failed to catch its name. All day it worried me and on the way back I had to get off the 'bus and see the name of the street. Then a house down the road would catch my eye and I would just have to look at that. Then a sign further on. Then a number.

I wandered on in a daze, staring like a madman at signs, numbers, street names, shop names, hoardings, trees, paving stones . . . anything. Hot, tired, sick to my stomach, light-headed, aware all the time that I was behaving insanely, I nevertheless went on with my compulsive urges.

I was mad. I would knock at people's houses to ask them if the place was to let, how much they wanted for the pram outside, whether their name was Smith, Jones, Brown or Robinson and, all the time, so conscious was I of acting abnormally, that I managed to make up good excuses and put on a face and act as though I were quite rational. To the best of my knowledge no one suspected that I was near total collapse — mental and physical collapse.

But once some kids in a street somewhere, began to follow me and shout after me. And once, when I was inspecting a field, a bare field, because I had been compelled to get off a train — a train, mind you — and walk back to this field and pick up a piece of paper in it and one piece of paper led to another and another till I was bent double crawling round the field picking up whatever caught my eye — once, then,

I was suddenly startled out of my wits by a big dog that leapt savagely at me and I screamed in terror while some workmen in the distance, who had observed my antics, laughed themselves near sick at having loosed the dog on me. I *was* sick. I vomited violently.

I would get home at nine or ten at night instead of at five p.m., weary to my finger tips, depressed, utterly utterly dejected and then have to make up lost time in my swotting.

I stopped sleeping. I toured the rooms at night fastening already fastened windows, turning off already locked gastaps, locking doors, putting the pieces of furniture in acceptable places, tidying my books, touching this, looking at that, till I wanted to cry aloud and collapse and die.

Why? Why, why, why, why, why, why, why . . . ? Because that inner voice told me I would fail if I did not do as I was being bidden.

And I couldn't fail. Mother did not even dream I could fail. No one believed I could fail. I had never failed anything yet. I was brilliant . . . so they said. A

337

genius. O God, what a pathetic genius! O God, help me in my misery!

I prayed. I mumbled. I besought. I cried to God. And all He said to me was *touch that and you won't fail . . . look at that and you will pass.*

I was even writing to inner dictation, crossing out words where they looked as if they did not fit, ending lines with words crammed by the dozen into tiny spaces or with big blank gaps, even making, actually making blots in certain places because I had to . . . I just had to, that's all.

There was a physical training mistress at college who took us, the males, in folk dancing through which we grimaced and mock-danced and had fun as we imitated pansy-boys and ballet dancers . . . and her. She was about thirty, perhaps a dozen years older than I, with a pleasing face and a very pretty figure. The chaps liked her, as a person and physically, too. They jostled one another to be invited to take tea with her. Once a week she had four or five of them in her room and they had tea. They would come back with tales of her round bottom as she bent away from them to lift the pot, of her short skirts (it was the days of very short skirts, remember) and her silken legs.

I was not bothered. I had too much on my mind to care.

But one day I received a tea invitation and on going up to her room one Friday evening found myself alone with her. We talked. She then asked me what was wrong, as if she knew.

I had kept the whole affair so bottled up within me that the realization that someone knew, someone cared, broke me completely. I began to tell her everything and was soon sobbing like a babe.

She put her arm round me to steady me and I went on with my story. I cried a lot, cried myself out and found her fingering my hair. And then, she taking the lead that I never would have done, I wasn't even thinking like that at the time, she put her soft face on mine and kissed me.

How it happened I do not know, I am not aware of the exact stages of the incident, but I do remember my fingers groping at her breasts and the way she put them into my hot, fumbling hands.

She made it easy for me. Then we were together and I had made my first woman. I was barely conscious what I was doing. I do not remember her, face or figure, or what I felt like. But I was with her, together as one, and still shaking with sobs as she shook with yearning. And we both trembled.

After that I was comforted, I remember. She promised to look after me. She told me to come to her whenever I felt like it. She would always be there to welcome me.

For two days I was nearly normal. I had at last found my manhood. And then I heard one of the other fellows boasting of having had a wilder, far more exciting passion-filled time with her than I had been able or willing or eager to have and I went away and wrapped myself sickly in unremitting gloom for many days.

And, after that, the neuroses returned a thousandfold. To avoid her I cut all lectures and worked in the Bethnal Green Library where it was quiet and managed, how I do not know, to get some studying done.

School Practice was a nightmare. I

succeeded in maintaining discipline in class but was faced, at one school in Peckham, with a disorderly crowd of youngsters after school who threw stones at me and made for me. I turned and ran. It was Blackboard Jungle years before the film was thought of.

To add to my sorrows I found myself suffering from a kind of inverted seeing — *hypnogoguic reaction*, I learned it was called later. Some people in advanced stages of cancer of the brain suffer from it. If I looked too long at an object it receded far, far away until I was seeing it through the powerful lens of an inverted telescope. The room I was in became unreal, like a surrealist nightmarish phantasy, and everything grew pinpoint in its clarity. If I stretched my hand out to touch something it was as if my hand was not part of me at all but another hand a million miles away. It was an unreal world I saw with unreal eyes.

Naturally enough I would close my eyes. And then the reverse happened. Whatever thoughts I thought, whatever my unseeing eyes saw, (and it is impossible to close the eyes and think of absolutely nothing) came right up and stood on my eyelids, monstrous, huge, terrifying. If I thought of fields, the grass stood like rugged oaks on my eyeball. If I thought of people they came and danced on my lids.

It was better to open them and peer at the distant over-clarified things around me than to close my eyes and have the unknown come up and hit me right in the centre of seeing.

The acuity of vision I perceived when looking with open eyes became a blurr of bare recognition when I closed them. Waking or trying to sleep, life became intolerable.

I had a constant headache. I was desperately, desperately tired. I was very sick. Physically and mentally ill. Yet no one knew at home. I hated them for not seeing my plight. Hated them all for not seeing what the physical training lecturess had seen. Or had she? Had she but desired me, poor, miserable, pathetic me? But she had given me solace and temporary comfort. Should I go back to college and see her perhaps?

But I was afraid. Afraid of consciously

having to make it clear that I wanted something — her, when it had come my way so unconsciously, so naturally, so unstrivingly, that it made me wonder, in my saner moments, why my friends and I and many others made so much fuss about so simple and natural and clean, yes clean, a human operation.

I didn't want it that unexciting. I wanted it with mad passion whenever I thought of her. And reason told me she was not like that. She gave herself without seduction, without passion, without clutchings and clawings and heavings, despite what that other fellow said. And I could not go back to college and go to her room and see her and sit and talk and wait for the moment to arrive in its own good time. I could not consciously do this without feeling a fraud and a cad. And so I was afraid to go back and see her.

I realize now that I should have done. She would have given me the consideration, the affection and then the love I was starving for.

But I didn't go.

And then I began to read backwards.

And as if this were not enough, to sit and stare at the end of my nose.

And yet I topped the whole college in the Psychology examination, scoring over ninety per cent while the next batch of students to me scored only seventy.

I topped the college again in a series of Intelligence Tests. I was told I had the IQ of a genius. I was living on my nerves alone and they were sustaining me. I was a genius gone mad.

I was ill, feverishly ill, and my examination papers were muddles of crossings out, blots, alterations and words written in between the lines, with huge gaps for no reason at all, all over the page. I was writing to a pattern that was forcing me to do weird and outrageous things.

Perhaps that was reckoned to be a sign of genius. For I took my examinations and turned my back on the college and went home.

Easier said than done. That evening I left college at about five p.m. The examinations were over. I would get me some much needed rest. But my tired body could not resist my mind at all, and my mind was devilish in its promptings. See that. Touch that. Look here. Go there. Figaro. Figaro, figaro, figaro, figaro, figaro, figaro, f-e-e-e-e . . . g-a-a-a-a-r . . . o-o-o-o-o. I was being called from all sides.

At nine I was lost somewhere south of the river and still following my nose. At eleven I didn't know where I was. I was quite overboard. All the too taut strings had at last snapped.

I collapsed in the Waterloo Road and a policeman helped me up and took me to the station. A doctor examined me and slowly I told him of my sufferings and anguish; of my voices and promptings.

He was a kindly, understanding man. He would not let me be sent to hospital, but insisted on driving me home and made me promise to tell someone, anyone, what was happening to me.

I stumbled in at one a.m. Mark turned over to ask me where I had been and I broke down and told him all.

Then things began to happen. My mother stood over me, wringing her hands, demanding to know why I hadn't said anything, hinted at my troubles to anyone. She didn't care if I failed. So I would take the exam again. She had suffered with me so long that it didn't matter if another year went by before I would be earning my keep.

And then I knew. Knew, knew what in part at least had made me what I then was. All through my college existence I was the "favoured" one. Nobody said it openly. It was hinted at. My brothers were keeping me. My mother was suffering so that I could go on and complete my education. And yet it was nothing like that. I had as much in scholarships as I was ever likely to earn when I got a job. In fact, during the first year of my first job I actually earned less than I had done at college: I had brought home more money in scholarships than I was to earn as a paid teacher.

I resented this patronizing. I never showed it, but deep down inside me resentment had built up, and this and my God Complex and my Guilt Complex and the stress of the examinations and the knowledge that I must not fail or I would let them all down and they'd all have to work to keep me for another long twelvemonth — all this had finally unbalanced me. But they were all to blame really. They and their patronage and the position they forced me into of having to be grateful, when there was no need at all to be grateful for anything.

Mark said we ought to get away. To a little place we knew near Pulborough under the shadow of the Sussex Downs. There we had spent many quiet wonderful days.

But peace did not come dripping slowly from gentle skies when we got there. I was still funking the result. In bed at night my heart began to palpitate like a threshing machine. The bed rocked. The room shook. Then I would want to go to the lavatory and as the W.C. was out in the garden I had to try and go in the pot and I could not with my brother watching me. So I sat there in the dark and the room began to smell and I would feel sick for Mark and vomit and get back into bed and the shaking would start all over again.

It was nightmare.

We went home. They put me to bed. But I fretted. I heard that my friends had failed. Four failures. Four Jews. Four bright students, too. Why only Jews? There had been marked anti-semitism at college. One or two of the lecturers had had unkind things to say about Jews. Was this a sign — even though more than one Professor had said to me: "You're not Jewish, are you? You play football and cricket." — O impossible combination!

I fretted. Then Mark and I went together to the college where I knew the lists were being posted three days before the students were informed by post.

I was afraid to scan the lists. But Mark found my name there — a safe, comfortable pass. I had done it. I looked and looked and even then had to make trebly sure my name wasn't being confused with another student's.

Two days later came the offer of a job from a dockside Education Committee and I was better. Miraculously I was better. I could resist impulses and scorn promptings and laugh at the little devil within me who nudged my mind and tugged at my brain.

I grew better rapidly. We went back to the little cottage in the shade of the

Sussex Downs and climbed the slopes and sat in the woods and found peace. And who could wish for a more understanding companion than my brother Mark who was then all things to me — father, brother, friend.

Thank you, Mark, for those peace-filled wonderful days. Thank you, O my brother, for your compassion, your wisdom and your big heart.

Fit again, I turned to teaching for a living and was soon writing my way into minor publication, too.

But a legacy has remained all the days of my life. I still get compulsions, though I can resist them. But I look at gastaps — as thousands upon thousands of ordinary people do. And I do not sleep well. It takes me hours to fall asleep. I used to worry, but I don't any more. So I don't sleep so well? Who cares? Edison could do with but a couple of hours a night, and Einstein with even less.

Sleep, the reconciler, the rest that peace begets, is an overrated psychological trick. If you want it desperately it eludes you. Snap your fingers at it and it comes.

Because I don't care whether I sleep or

not I find sleep more and more willing to embrace me. I sleep better now than I ever did at any stage of my life.

I give you now the cure of cures for insomnia. Welcome wakefulness and ye shall sleep.

It is the only cure, the finest cure. I know. And I give it to you here and now for your own experimentation. Try it.

Realization comes like an awakening from a bad dream. "Brother, do you think you're in trouble? Then look at me!" Only now in reverse. For the slums he didn't, as a child, know that he, as a child, inhabited; for the slums that he, as a youth, knew he inhabited and was ashamed of; these slums he saw, as a man, were not slums at all when compared with his later discoveries of far worse conditions.

Everything is comparable to something else. When he knew this he knew that life itself is a comparison and the act of self-being is only valid when compared with others' existences.

So, in the full flush of manhood, realization dawned, that his sufferings were not extreme. That others had suffered worse. That money doesn't buy success, fame and happiness. That Jews are not all good even if they aren't all bad. That even maybe somewhere somehow there is a good German. That not all grass is green and not all love sex. Nothing is absolute and, similarly, nothing is null and voidful. One can almost believe with Tennyson that: "Not

351

a moth in vain desire is shrivelled in a fruitless fire." When one believes that one has glimpsed the countenance of the Godhead.

So, as he grew into the maturity, he began to find himself. And is this not the purpose of life's journey; namely, to find oneself? For perhaps if a man find himself he may then also find a short cut to God.

29

Dockside

I THOUGHT we lived in a slum till I saw the dockside area of London. Let me qualify that. Until I was fifteen or sixteen I did not think Broughton Buildings was a tenement or Goolden Street a slum. After that I thought it was. When I began to teach at the age of twenty-one or -two I knew Broughton Buildings was in a slum area and that there were other parts of London that were worse, but until I began to teach in Custom House, near the West Ham docks, I did not know how much worse.

Goolden Street and Broughton Buildings was a fairy-land compared with the neighbourhood in which I found myself teaching school. Most of the children, dirty and unclean, came to school in bare feet in the summer; and even in the winter some of the children of the Irish dockers ran the streets in bare feet.

Literacy was at such a low ebb that we had boys leaving school at fourteen whom we could never teach to read. Others stumbled and mumbled a halting way through one-syllabled three-and four-letter words without ever making sense of the simplest sentences.

The teachers slaved at their tasks. Reading lessons went on through most of the day with backward readers. Teachers gave up their spare time to hold classes for handfuls of dumb kids.

Arithmetic was not such a problem. There were children who could not read a word yet could figure easily and rapidly; but give them a problem in words and they were stuck. They gazed at you blankly.

Then they would look at you wistfully, up would go their hands and they would ask: "Is it adding up or taking away, sir?" Once you told them, they could do it in a flash.

Little baldheaded Harnetty, whose parents believed in giving him a monk's tonsure, could neither read, write nor figure. No good at the Three Rs, no good at games, no good it seemed at anything, this thin, semi-starved lad was yet likeable enough because he was such a nice natured kid. One evening I went to the Dog Track at West Ham and bought a programme. I tendered the kid a ten-shilling note and there was Harnetty, counting out the right change to a penny and doing it all the time.

When I asked him next day why he could not take away *2d.* from a shilling yet could do it with programmes, he was too bemused to answer. He couldn't tell me why. But I could tell him. Sums as set in class bore no relation to the world in which these children lived. Give them sums they had to do in their daily tasks and they would do them. I experimented along these lines. Harnetty never became an Einstein; yet by the end of the year he could add up simple numbers and subtract simpler ones. But he never learned to read.

Reading was so difficult for these children because it was an unnatural thing. Their fathers and mothers didn't read. There were no books in the house. The daily newspaper, if there was one, was merely a preselected dog-or horse-racing programme, an early edition of the afternoon or evening's runners.

In the morning most of the children were tired and sleepy. All of them did extra jobs after school, though they were but nine and ten years old.

They ran errands. They sold papers. They chopped wood. They sold programmes. They pushed carts. By the time they were eleven or twelve they were working pretty regularly at these odd jobs and it was school and schooling which were the breaks and not vice versa. With fathers out of work and mothers finding charing and scrubbing hard to come by, these kids not only had to work but were often depended on for the couple of shillings a week they brought home.

Tired in the morning, they went off at twelve o'clock and were back in the playground at ten past with a piece of bread and dripping in their hands. Some of them did not go home at all. They took a dried crust from their pockets, drank at the school tap and were supposedly content.

They had never tasted butter — "Cor, sir, it makes yer sick," said one who had. They never had new clothes. They wore their fathers' or elder brothers' cut-me-downs. They never got spending money. They were supposed to find this for themselves and it was a wonder, in these circumstances, that there was not more delinquency. They stayed away from school on the slightest pretext, sometimes for weeks at a stretch. The most overworked man in the district was the school attendance officer. They were lousy, bug-and flea-infested, and many of them suffered from nasty sores and suppurations.

I used to compare them with the children I knew at Broughton Buildings and I wondered why it was that the children of just as poor parents were better fed and better dressed and better cared for.

Not that the answer was hard to find. For one thing, in the Ghetto any money that came into a house was the joint property of the entire family. Food was number-one item on the bill. Clothes and personal care next. But in these dockside

357

Gentile families any money that came into the house was the father's, even if the wife had earned it. First and foremost consideration were the pints of beer that could be bought every night at the pub; men would spend more each night in the local than they earned during the day. After beer, the next item was betting — sixpenny doubles and shilling cross doubles and threepenny trebles mounted up to five or six shillings a day, far more than they were earning. And the result was that there was no money left in the house for food; and, if there was, then the food was the old man's first, and the scraps went to the mother and kids.

There was no family love, no family ties, no family kinship. I am speaking generally, of course, and there were exceptions; but they were so rare. Parents didn't care what happened to their children. Children talked scathingly about their old man and old woman.

Up in the staff room I also found myself in a strange world. Here were men who talked only of the day of retirement and could calculate precisely what they would be earning in three, five or ten years. Life was fixed for them. Now they looked forward to its end.

For me this was terrible, a very negation of living that I found intolerable. These men were not only in a rut — they were in their own graves and digging them deeper with each day that passed.

They came fresh from college, eager to set the world to rights and, within a few months, were as fast in the rut as their colleagues. Poorly paid — the starting wage for a college trained teacher was then thirteen pounds thirteen shillings a month — they awaited with eagerness their increment of twelve pounds a year and after that of another twelve pounds a year, so that they knew that in five years' time they would be earning another sixty pounds a year and they looked forward hopefully, with tremendous anticipation, to those better-monied days. When the days came they were worse off than ever; by the time they were earning £250 a year they were married and had taken upon themselves the usual family commitments.

Again, these men, like the children, went short of good food and clothes.

They were neat and clean, but somewhat shabbily so. Their lunch consisted of sandwiches or ham rolls that they sent out for. Or they would bring their lunch with them and cook it over the school common room gas ring.

I shuddered for the lives they led. So narrow was their field of vision that when, once a month, they banded together to visit the West End, they called it "going up to London". Where then did they think they lived? In the wilds of Alaska or Timbuctoo?

There was strife in the common room, too. They, the elder ones, were intolerant of the younger ones. In this period between the wars some of them resented the fact that they had to fight in the First World War and were always saying to us younger ones: "Do you good when the next one comes — you'll know what we went through."

And one young schoolteacher, O'Shaughnessy, an Irishman with whom I became friendly, fell foul of them just because he was Irish and they happened to hate the Micks. One day there were blows struck in the common room.

They were not very partial to Jews either, but they tolerated me. When I had been to Jewish weddings I would bring them cigars; and I brought them jars of roll mops, pickled cucumbers, gherkins and bottled delicatessen that my mother-in-law to be would give me to give them as a treat. They liked these additions to their diet. But when, one day, I brought them a jar of olives, not one of them had ever tasted them before, and they refused to sample them. O'Shaughnessy took one bite and spat the olive out in disgust.

I gave them these things because I liked to give. There was no ulterior motive.

Sometimes I brought sandwiches. Smoked salmon . . . they would not believe it. They thought I was a millionaire. Yet they all had more money than I did, more than my fiancée's parents, more than my family had. We could afford smoked salmon fairly often. They never even dreamed of buying it. Why? What's the answer?

I found that they lived in tight little worlds where the pocket was always their master. Money meant far more to them than it did to us. They scrimped to save. One teacher, who had through the years bought property and was comfortably provided for, rode to school each day a distance of thirty miles, on his bicycle, wore shiny suits and patched shirts and his lunch consisted of two ham rolls. Yet, compared with all the people I knew, he was wealthy. And when I spoke, tactlessly I must admit, about a bottle of wine in the house or ate smoked salmon sandwiches and smoked large cigarettes instead of the whiffs they smoked, he and the rest of them thought I was rolling in money. They were envious of *me*!

My clothes were better than theirs. My shirts were not whiter perhaps but wholier. I had few pennies but I never thought about them and when occasion demanded would contribute to funds or give a kid a copper for running an errand for me while they held tightly on to every ha'penny. My mother had taught me that someone needed my last penny more than I did myself.

Time and time again my theory was proven that the English Gentile is the meanest man on earth. Perhaps tightest is a better word, for it suggests also the limited aspect of his entire seeing, his narrow mindedness, his over-concern for the future and the way he suffers the present for a tomorrow that, even if it comes, is too full of fears to be enjoyed.

It was the Jew, generally supposed to be mean, who was free with his money and lived for the day and had a much broader, much less inhibited outlook.

Biased? It would be natural for me to be so. But the bias cuts both ways. I have been accused by my own people of being anti-semitic. Many of us are. We hate the show, the flashiness, the gaudiness, the over-dressiness to which some of us are prone.

I detest that in Jews that makes them want to shine in any company; I abhor the fur-wrapped fat women parading to synagogue, the diamonds on the hands of the men, the loud voices, the over-emphatic gestures. I have ranted about these time and again. I have been told I am an enemy and a traitor to my kind. Maybe I am.

I know our faults too well. But let this

suggestion of wealth be not mistaken. Many of the Jews you see around you who look as if they are millionaires are no wealthier than you. They are merely spending their money today and you are so carefully saving for tomorrow; and often they have spent tomorrow's money, too, before they have earned it.

Money is a means of enjoyment to the Jew. He wants it because he understands and loves living. He likes good food, good clothes, the appurtenances of wealth. Give him ten pounds and he will spend eleven. Give the Gentile ten pounds and, having spent four of them on beer, he will save five and live on the rest.

I dislike flashy Jews. I dislike the gown manufacturing kings who have made money and love to show it. I think they are gross, boorish and a disgrace to our race. I detest the cosmetic kings even more; for they have a superficial air and an unhealthy grace which barely conceals their gutter manners.

A cosmetic king once said to me during a discussion on music: "There is only one instrument — that's the violin. The rest are not worth a light." And all his fawning hearers agreed.

I was mad with rage. I knew something, more than most I fancy, about violin playing. I worshipped the maestros. I loved their playing. But I knew that they themselves would be the last to declare that the violin was the only instrument in the orchestra and I certainly would never have made so blind, so rash a statement.

Had I not wept when Joseph played? The violin, it was *my* instrument. On its notes I soared to the very gateways of heaven.

But because this gross fat man was a cosmetic king, it gave him the right to pronounce judgement on things he knew nothing about. He made his statement, *ex cathedra*, categorically, arbitrarily, and he was listened to with respect and agreement because he was powerful and wealthy.

This sort of thing I hate. It makes me squirm. Around many wealthy Jews there is a coterie of Yes-men and servile arselickers who make this man think he is even mightier than he thinks himself to be.

I cannot stand the power-pushing complex of some Jews who create anti-semitism. There are enough Eichmanns in this world without the Jews themselves having to create more.

But not all Jews are rich. Most of them are like most Gentiles, poor, not so poor, comfortable and wealthy. Some of them are very poor. And, to offset this false aristocracy of wealth there is still, and I hope there always will be, the aristocracy of learning that has carried the Jew through the centuries to artistic, scientific, musical and cultural achievement.

When next you think of the monied Jews who look like fat pigs and act like them too . . . when next you think of a Streicher cartoon, think for a moment of Sara Bernhardt and Alicia Markova and, yes, even of Jesus Christ, and you will see that beauty and grace and godliness are not essentially Gentile virtues; think too of the great ones of literature, science, music, painting, sculpting, acting, playwriting. Think not only of Levi the Gown Manufacturer and Cohen of cosmetics, but of Levi the artist and Cohen the great judge. When next you want to condemn the boor, think of Epstein and Elman and Heifetz and Menuhin and Lord Samuel, one of the wisest men of the age, and Einstein and Arthur Miller and Al Jolson and of the three who made modern music: Kern, Gershwin and Berlin, and thousands of others.

When you think of the gross uneducated peasants flaunting their wealth and bad manners, think also of the intelligent, delicate, cultured ones who are so, so different. Like everyone else we are a mixture of good and bad. Why is it that only the bad are noticed? For every fat cosmetic king driving about in his splendid Rolls-Royce there are a thousand good musicians in good orchestras up and down the country eking out a meagre living because they love their art; for every swollen-bellied gown manufacturer who can't speak the Queen's English without foulness, coarseness and obscenity, there are a thousand pale-eyed scientists and mathematicians working behind the scenes in anonymity, a thousand research doctors pledging their lives to the cure of mankind's illnesses and diseases.

Why does the fat, overblown, over-dressed Jew catch the eye? Why? He is so much in the minority. He is not really representative of Jews as a race.

Be tolerant with us. We are as you, good and bad alike, breathing, eating, sleeping and mating as you do. We are human, that's all.

Yet my colleagues in the staff common room thought all Jews were fat and wealthy. I was slim. I played games with the kids and the kids loved me for it. I was a freak. There could not be any more like me. Jews were fat. Jews were rich. Jews were mean. They said Jews were mean. It *killed* me.

My brother Mark used to give me hand-made cigarettes that his future mother-in-law made for special people. Some of them had gold tips. I brought a handful to the common room and gave them away. They seized them with avidity. Lit up. Inhaled. Sat back and felt like kings.

I said, by way of making conversation: "That's real gold round the tip. Finely beaten tissue-paper-thin real gold leaf. I wonder how many it would take before they made an inch thick nugget of real gold . . . "

And two of the men to whom I had just given five cigarettes apiece lifted their hands above their ears and shook them to and fro in what they thought was a typically Jewish gesture. "Oi veh . . . " said one; "Oi-yoi-yoi," said the other, and they waggled their hands at me forwards and backwards beside their ears.

That I had given them cigarettes, they forgot. That I had given them jars of delicatessen, they forgot. That I had given them cigars, they forgot. That I had paid their fares on trams and that they had never paid mine, they forgot.

They remembered only that I was Jewish.

And all Jews were mean.

They were not unkindly people. They were educated to a fair standard. Good with children. Hard-working and conscientious. Like me, they had been the bright boys of their schooldays and had been forced into teaching because there was very little else a poor boy could do in those days.

Like the boys I knew, these co-teachers of mine had not been called to teaching. They were not men with a vocation. But, unlike the boys I knew, they had also considered that teaching gave them a social status that lifted them out of their artisan and labouring background into the professional classes.

Jewish boys it seemed did not think about social class when they took up teaching. They thought about their parents and the sacrifices that had been made for them and essayed teaching as a means of bringing money into the home sooner than one could do it by becoming a doctor or a lawyer.

But these teachers were class conscious. They had raised themselves out of their backgrounds and at the time I knew them were all voting staunchly Conservative; not because they were true blue so much as the fact that by voting Tory they differentiated themselves immediately from the lower classes.

Poor in-a-rut unfortunates. I felt sorry for them. Their mean little worlds would have stifled me. I began to write. And as soon as some small success came my way

I threw up teaching. Times were better. Jobs were not so scarce.

I heard from them occasionally, particularly when a new book of mine was published and they saw the reviews or came across it in their public libraries.

Then, with the coming of the second great war, they were dispersed over the country. The dirty little school, with its two-by-four playground that was not nearly as large as the Broughton Buildings Arch, and its dirty little classrooms received a direct hit and became a mass of rubble.

Since no one was killed I consider this the one good thing the Luftwaffe did. When Hitler comes to be judged he can truthfully say: I was responsible for getting rid of that filthy little school down by the London Docks.

O'Shaughnessy is still alive. He is now Headmaster of another Dockside school. And he, the ambitious, the eager, the young adventurer who thought (as I did) that teaching was a digging of one's own grave and that teachers were arrested developers who never progressed beyond a standard eighteen years of living and maturity, is now the deadliest bore I ever knew. A typical narrow-minded teacher if ever I saw one. But a nice chap, still. Kindly. Tolerant. But not wise. Not wise. You can't be wise when your life is given over to teaching, since your world is limited and your horizons so closely defined. Beauty becomes a dream and your visions of it pass and are replaced by the ruled lines of the curriculum and the dust on the blackboard.

Teaching is a great and noble profession. But only a small mind can stand it for long.

30

Together Again

THEY did not all die, the sweet remembered ones. Many were left, are left. These I have disguised, even though I have nothing but good words for all of them. For who knows? unlike me they may not be pleased to be reminded of their background.

Olim meminisee juvabit. Some time it may be pleasing to remember the way you turned your head; your hair, your eyes, your laughter; but it is anguish now.

Never for me. Only understanding. And wisdom.

One of my school friends who shall be nameless, for he does not fit into this scheme of things at all, went on to make a name for himself in the City, to head a large business and employ lots of people. When I used to see him and we went walking towards our appointed lunch, he refused to recognize old acquaintances. Not that we saw them at every corner. But now and again, once or twice a year, someone would pass, a familiar face would turn at us, and my friend went on, unheeding. "Why do you always write," he asked me once, "about the East End? Why can't you forget your past? You suffer from a form of inverted snobbery!" Ah me, there are words for everything these days. No one thinks straight any more. If you do, you are suffering from thinkingstraightitis. I stopped lunching with this old friend. He was a good, intelligent, honourable man. But he was ashamed of his background. I am not proud of it, but I am not unproud of it, either. And I am unhappy with anyone who is ashamed of those bad days and those good people.

I do not live in the past. I am too concerned with the daily business of living. It is quite a business, too, this rat race that humanity runs.

Ah, my beloved, fill the cup that
  clears
Today of past regrets and future
  fears:
Tomorrow! — why tomorrow I may
  be
Myself with yesterday's sev'n thousand
  years.

Memory is deep. And round me dwell the shadows of the past. And today is not today because today would never have been without all those yesterdays. And tomorrow belongs to the past as I pray it may belong to my future. Life is a collection of memories. What we think, what we feel, what we are stems from what we thought, felt and did and how we acted half a second ago and an hour ago and a month ago and ten years ago and a lifetime ago. Living is progressive dying, progressive from split second to split second, a pyramid of breathings held at the base by our mother's womb.

I can turn inwardly and see myself when young. My beloved Booba and Zaida stand closest. And around them presses a throng, the living and the dead, united in youth, united in perhaps their only immortality, in the immortality of my thoughts and, after I have gone, in the deathless remembrance of others who will see them again and thus remember.

Shall I deny my dear ones their immortality? Stop myself from growing? For growing young is as easy or as hard as growing old and though the body finds it more and more difficult to achieve, the mind compensates by making it more simple with every passing year.

They stand around me. The father I hardly knew. Am I like you at all, father? Booba and Zaida. Jack Dripper. I got a vitness for bollocks. Axelrodt: sedan, sedan. Hewson: and suppose Life is not like a fish? Jerry Short who lived like a swift swallow-flight of song and died all too soon. Uncle Adolf: come, come, come to me, Thora. I stand once again in the Northland, but in silence and in shame; your grave is my only landmark, and men have forgotten your name. Come to me, Thora. Cousin Lionel who now sleeps with the fishes deep in the ocean's chill bosom: ding, dong, bell, poor Lionel.

Cousin Lionel who farted in bed. And Smelly, who did the same thing in his school clothes. Allen the patriot turned Red turned patriot in death. Harry! the voice from the past, almost the dead past — the tattered old autograph album and my tears falling. Laughing Shorty. Elegant Hyman. Kindly old man Lewis. Blind Pete: what's blue, what's red, what's yellow? Lucky to be alive, indeed. Brother Ben singing Brown Bird to the imperishable notes of a violin played by Joseph Kauffman. O that incomparable talent. And Henry Klutzak painting the trite, the commonplace, the dreary and stroking it to wonder and beauty and poetry.

Poetry and my good friend and mentor, Mr. Evans. Sleep well in your Welsh hills, O my shepherd and guide. Bully pinching backsides black and blue. What rosy cherubs sit across your fat thighs and squeal to your thumb twists? A donnage of Oxford professors breaking a boy's heart because all the Greek he could say was rosy-fingered dawn. In the beginning God created the Heaven and the earth. And the earth was without form and void.

And there was darkness upon the face of the deep. And God said let there be light and there was light. O wonderful poetry in Hebrew and even more wondrous in that stern, beautiful monosyllabic English.

My friends and companions, Tennyson, Browning, Keats, Shakespeare, Francis Thompson, Donne, Housman, the Rosettis. All as alive to me as though they had been members of my family. Byron too and Swinburne and Shelley and a host of the lesser-known wordsmiths who made the language sing. Wolfe, Hemingway, Saroyan.

My brothers, my sisters — God spare them. And my mother. My amazing mother. Mother of so many. Kirschenbaum loving her. Even Blackie Ferret giving her respect.

The whores, the prozzies, the pimps, the touts, but no perverted. O my salaciously clean East End. Are you a Jew? Prove it. First time unlucky. Poor Jackie. Poor Gussy. How many times have you been clapped since then?

All, all the old familiar faces.

There they are my many men and

women. Where the heart lies let the brain lie also.

Dead? Who says so?

In every breath, in every thought as fast as the speed at which light could think, in every murmur of my being they are there, large and strong and alive. I have not given them life. I have tried to bring them a little substance and shade. To me they are, have, always will be exultantly ecstatically thrillingly alive.

How old are the hills and the buds that break? What is age? They do not grow old, my East Enders. For me they remain as they were, unaltered, unchanging in a changing world.

Come up into the streets again with me, O my young companions. Return to our lost world, come back and haunt me no more. Come back as I first knew you in that timeless stretch of youth when the days were long and the hearts were young and laughter fell like ripe plums from trees kissed by a fabulous summer. Out of the dingy flats into the grey streets where we could poke a finger into the stars and twirl the clouds around our heads. Where the tenements were silvern palaces and the music of the day engulfed them and the whole of living was one vibrant voice that cried upon us to mix with it and be of it and share with it the ecstasy of being.

Grey was the East End and pearl grey its skies and golden its days and lit with purpled splendour its hustling nights. Come with me and let's play again, live again, talk again, grudge sleep again.

O where are they now, the lost souls, the lost years? Around me. About me. In dreaming. Come, then, out into the world of unreality and into this phantom day of present and let us reverse-spin the globe and dance with the quick, shining earth as it carries us back into dream pastures that stay bright for us. Come again into the timeless past you who are dead and you who live and let us meet again, the living with all the ghosts of the past, and be as we were.

And the wind moans through the bare streets, on the blank street a thousand bald days break, and the shadow of Broughton Buildings rises up towards a dead sky and once again we feed a poverty that was riches and a slum that was beautiful. Music rushes through the narrow alleyways and the area railings shake with dancing and the old school hall is shoulder packed with those who were and are and all who have never died return again into the enchanted slum and stand, savouring the miraculous wonder of it.

Ah youth, lost and windborne. Ah the friends, the family, the dear ones, the departed. Ah those voices from the dead past. Come again, lost ones, forever lost, forever living.

Come and haunt me now and through eternity.

*It was time to leave the East End.
Time to quit Broughton Buildings. We
had grown too good for it. We were not
children any longer. Lily, the youngest,
was over seventeen, I nearly twenty,
Ben twenty-two, Betty twenty-four, Mark
twenty-six. Polly, my eldest sister, and
Edward, my eldest brother, were married
and had children. Mother was a grandmother thrice over.*

*Nothing kept us there but sentiment.
And dear friends.*

*We packed our meagre belongings, and
watched by a crowd of sorrowing people,
many of them sobbing openly, our van
began to move off.*

*We stood at the back and waved.
Practically every inhabitant of Broughton
Buildings waved back at us. Those who
were not on the ground to see us off
waved and shouted at us from upstairs
windows. Nobody ever had a better
send off.*

*We waved till the van turned a corner
and we lost sight of the crowd.*

★ ★ ★

Good-bye East End. Good-bye Broughton Buildings. Good-bye friends. And farewell youth. Farewell my youth. Farewell the years, the sorrows, the heartaches, the pain and the living, and with it all the joy.

Farewell forever. There is no turning back. Only in memory. Only in memory.

The van rumbled on towards our new home many miles away. And no one said a word . . .

TO FIGHT THE WILD
Rod Ansell and Rachel Percy

Lost in uncharted Australian bush, Rod Ansell survived by hunting and trapping wild animals, improvising shelter and using all the bushman's skills he knew.

COROMANDEL
Pat Barr

India in the 1830s is a hot, uncomfortable place, where the East India Company still rules. Amelia and her new husband find themselves caught up in the animosities which seethe between the old order and the new.

THE SMALL PARTY
Lillian Beckwith

A frightening journey to safety begins for Ruth and her small party as their island is caught up in the dangers of armed insurrection.